Tom Slemen
LIVERPOOL
GHOST WALK

© Tom Slemen 2005

Published by The Bluecoat Press, Liverpool
Book design by MARCH Graphic Design Studio, Liverpool
Printed by Graham & Heslip

ISBN 1 904438 34 2

Tom Slemen
LIVERPOOL
GHOST WALK

The Bluecoat Press

CONTENTS

INTRODUCTION

In October 2003, I conducted Liverpool's first-ever ghost walk. This came about when the *Daily Post* ran a competition in which the twenty winners were to be taken by me around Liverpool on a tour of the city's ghostly hot-spots.

On a cold autumnal morning, *Daily Post* columnist Peter Elson and the twenty eager prize winners rendezvoused with me at Central Station, from there I took them on a two-hour guided walk which stretched from Bold Street, to St Luke's Church, encompassing half of Rodney Street and finishing up in that gothic dormitory of the Victorian dead, St James's Cemetery. The walk was a resounding success, for which I received much applause in the twilit graveyard.

When news of the ghost tour was reported in the *Post*, about a dozen people contacted me by email and snail-mail, wanting to know when the next ghost walk was due to take place. I had regarded the competition as a one-off event but I finally gave in to public pressure, and, rather naively, stated in the *Liverpool Echo* that I would be at the Paradise Street bus station at a certain time and date, and if anyone was interested in participating in another ghost and mystery sightseeing tour, they only had to turn up. I only expected about twenty to thirty people to show any interest, at best.

I reached the station at the appointed time and found the place thronged with people, whom I assumed to be waiting for buses. Not sure who, if any of them, had come for the walk, I turned to a random group of people and announced that I was about to start the Liverpool Ghost Walk. Almost everyone present – an estimated five hundred people – turned towards me and formed themselves into a massive circle. They stood looking at me expectantly and I realised that I had better do something pretty quickly.

Summoning all the lung capacity I could muster, I addressed them at the top of my voice. I told them that I had not expected anything like that number of people to turn up, and tried to explain that it would be impossible to take everyone on the tour. The crowd just looked at me blankly and every last one of them stubbornly insisted on joining the tour. I was left with very little choice but to leave the bus station with hundreds of people in tow, feeling like the Pied Piper of Hamblin. I expected to be arrested at any minute for causing a public disturbance, and in Church Street, a police van crawled through the crowd and from its passenger window a stern-looking policeman said to me, "Are you Tom Slemen?"

My stomach turned over, but I meekly answered, "Yes."

"Have you ever heard about a ghost that haunts a police station in Woolton?" the policeman said, and the driver of the vehicle stopped the van and also leaned towards the passenger side, eager to hear my reply.

I reeled off what I knew of the haunted police station, and expected the policeman to then take me into custody, but after I had related my tale about a ghostly constable, the crowd following me surged forward, sweeping me along with them. I stood on a bollard in the thoroughfare and addressed the crowd, which had now become even bigger, as other people joined in the tour when they learned who I was and what we were doing.

One youth swore at me and said, "I don't believe in ghosts. It's all a load of rubbish!" That youth was almost lynched by two tough-looking shaven-headed men who had recently joined in the tour. The menacing duo told the heckler he would find out from first-hand experience if there was an after-life if he didn't beat it, and the cynic quickly scuttled away.

There was something almost Biblical about the way in which the multitude followed me every step of the way, hanging on my every word – up Church Street and down Church Alley to the courtyard of Bluecoat Chambers. By this time the crowd must have numbered about six hundred. One man, at the front of the crowd, who knew all of the tales in my *Haunted Liverpool* books by heart, kept finishing my sentences for me as I related a tale about a certain window at the Bluecoat. That man was treated to a barrage of insults and threats by the enormous crowd.

"Hey, mate, let the man speak, will you? We haven't come to listen to you."

"Yeah! Clear off if you can't keep your mouth shut."

And so it went on.

In Hanover Street, part of the crowd temporarily broke away and almost crushed into the Neptune Theatre, where people were already queuing on the stairs for tickets to the musical *Grease*. Then the crowd completely obstructed Bold Street, and I stood on the steps of the Lyceum, relating, at the top of my voice, the many tales of timeslips in that part of the street. Security guards from a nearby store, who had come to listen to the stories from the entrance to their premises, nodded in agreement as I talked about the ghostly Victorian hansom cab that had recently been seen near Concert Street. A courting couple at the back of St Luke's Church received a terrific shock when I arrived on the scene with nearly seven hundred people in tow. I told several tales about the church and an assortment of paranormal incidents which had taken place within its precincts, then moved on to Rodney Street – the haunting ground of Mr McKenzie from the pyramid – and ultimately to St James's Cemetery, where the crowd gathered around the Mount to hear the legend of Ginny Greenteeth.

Finally, the vast assembly of ghost seekers encircled Huskisson's Tomb, where a hush descended as I described the limping spectre who haunted the cemetery. By then, over two hours had passed, and my throat was getting quite sore. The most popular walk in Liverpool's history came to an end, and a huge cheer echoed throughout the cemetery.

As the mass gathering began to break up into groups, I realised that, unless the number of people attending any future ghost walk could be regulated (a very difficult task), then this would have to be the first and last walk of its kind. This seemed a pity as there was obviously a great deal of interest in it. It was then that I decided that a *Haunted Liverpool Ghost Walk* guidebook would be the ideal way for those interested in local hauntings and tales of mystery to embark on their very own personal tour. Armchair reading is all very well, but a practical guidebook would give the reader a chance to get out and actually explore the very places where ghosts walk, as well as visiting the strange scenes and sinister localities described in my *Haunted Liverpool* stories.

Here then, is a street guide to the gothic, the ghoulish and the ghostly places of *Haunted Liverpool*. It is a map of mystery and marvel, not to be undertaken lightly, for the paths lead through the domain of demons, vampires, ghosts, doppelgangers and banshees. Being part of a group on a guided tour of a city's supernatural haunts is unnerving enough, but embarking on the *Haunted Liverpool Ghost Walk* alone, or in small numbers, will most definitely be a strain for even the most hardened sceptic's nervous system!

A few words of warning before you begin the ghost tour. If you intend to venture out by night to visit the places on the ghost walk, then do not go alone into secluded locations, because Liverpool, like any other major city in the world, is haunted by muggers and other criminals who are at large after dark.

Now we have dispensed with the caution, It only remains for me to wish you good ghost hunting!

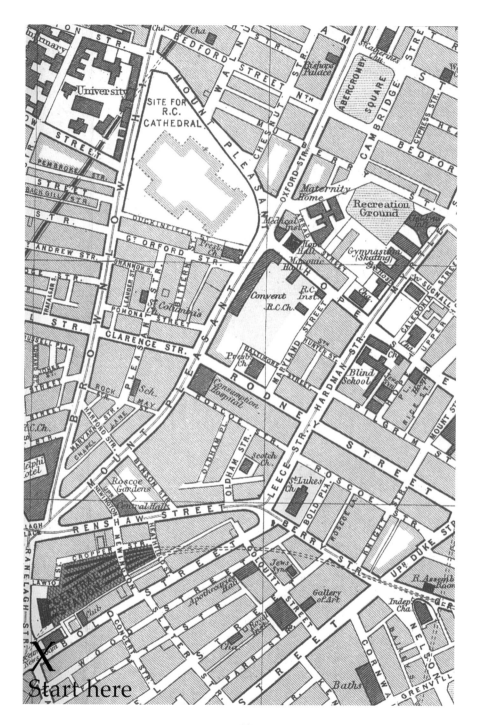

X

Start here

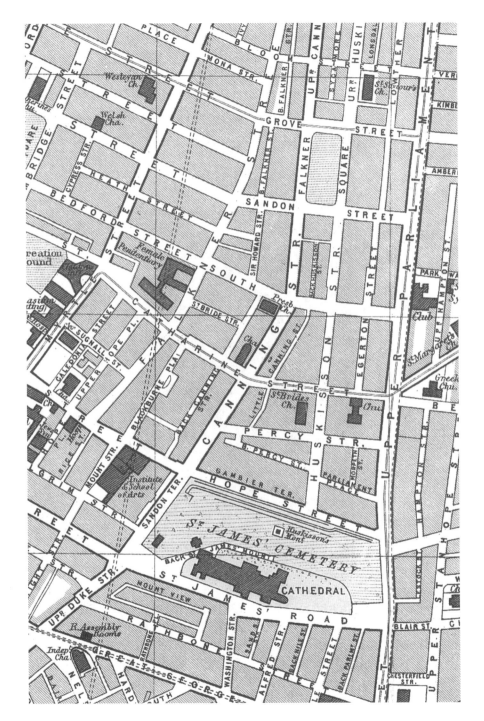

CENTRAL STATION

Begin the ghost walk on the incline which leads from Central Station to the bottom of Bold Street with the Lyceum building on your right. This particular location has been the scene of several intriguing timeslips.

BOLD STREET TIMESLIP

One blazing hot July Saturday afternoon in 1996, Frank, an off-duty policeman from Melling and his wife Carol, had travelled to Liverpool for a shopping trip. At Central Station the couple split up. Carol set off to what was then Dillons bookshop in Bold Street to purchase a copy of Irvine Welsh's book, *Trainspotting*, while Frank headed for a record store in Ranelagh Street, to try and find a CD he'd been looking for.

About twenty minutes later he was walking up the incline from the railway station when everything suddenly went unnaturally quiet. He then found himself stepping back in time into what seemed to be a rainy day in postwar Liverpool. A box van, with the name Caplan's emblazoned on its side, narrowly missed the time-displaced policeman, its horn blaring. This struck Frank as doubly odd as the bottom of Bold Street had been pedestrianised for some time and van's like that had disappeared years ago.

Frank walked on in shock across the cobbled road, intending to go and meet up with his wife in Dillon's (now occupied by Waterstones). Instead, he found a store called Cripps on the site of the Bold Street bookshop, with a large display of ladies handbags and shoes in the window. Frank scanned the street and noticed that all the people were wearing clothes which belonged to the 1940s and 50s, which really unnerved him. He realised that he had somehow walked into the Bold Street of forty-odd years ago.

Suddenly, Frank spotted a young woman who was very definitely dressed in the fashion of the mid-1990s – hipster jeans and a sleeveless top and carrying a Miss Selfridge bag – and he realised that she must have also somehow strolled into the past. This was comforting but it was still a paradox. He smiled at the girl as she walked past him and into Cripps.

As he followed her through the entrance doors, the whole interior of the building changed in a flash, back to that of Dillons bookshop. The people all around him were once again dressed in up to date clothes and were either browsing through the books which were displayed on the tables, or scanning the bookshelves for the particular volume they were after. Without considering what he was doing, he grabbed the girl by the arm.

"Did you see that?" he asked her.

"Yeah. I thought it was a new shop that had just opened. I was going to look at the clothes, but it's a bookshop," she said calmly. She did not seem to think there was anything frightening in what had happened, although she acknowledged that it was rather odd.

She then just laughed, shook her head and walked back out again. Frank later described how the girl had looked back and shaken her head again in disbelief. When he told his wife about the incident, she said that she had not noticed anything strange about the shop, or the street, but Frank was completely adamant that he had not hallucinated the episode.

I gave an account of this incident on the *Billy Butler Show* on local radio. Within minutes people were ringing in to the station to confirm that, in the late 1950s and early 1960s, there had been a store called Cripps, situated in the exact location where the bookshop now stood. I also discovered that a firm called Caplan's was in existence in the same time frame as Cripps and did indeed use box vans of the type that Frank encountered during his baffling experience. What's more, I also received many letters and telephone calls from listeners who had also experienced strange things in the same part of Bold Street where the policeman had stepped into another era.

Months before this timeslip, workmen renovating the Lyceum building experienced an inexplicable time loss, and one workman's digital watch went backwards for two hours before his very eyes. On another occasion he put down his safety helmet and when he looked down, seconds later, it was gone, yet there was no one within fifty feet of him.

CONCERT STREET

Carry on up Bold Street – in the direction of St Luke's bombed out church, which is visible at the top of the street – and cross over to the right-hand side of the street, to Concert Street. This street forms part of a square and is so-called because the grand building on its left side, with a row of pillars at its entrance, was once the Liverpool Music Hall, where hundreds of concerts were held in Victorian and Edwardian times. If you look high above the Bold Street entrance you will find a clue to this building's past in the engraved motto 'HALLES DES MODES'. This building has a long history of hauntings.

MUSIC HALL MYSTERIES

In the 1970s, a lady dressed in a long, dark, crinoline dress, was often spotted gliding about the ground floor of the building, early in the morning. Some people who encountered the ghostly woman described her as having a very melancholy appearance and one witness said he heard what seemed to be the same ghost crying, again in the morning time. Her identity is still unknown.

In 2001 and 2003, there were two fascinating sightings of a group of ghosts at the rear of the former music hall building, on Wood Street. If you look at the rear of the building you will see a row of pillars. Leaning against these pillars, at around midnight, one evening in October 2001, were three men dressed in old fashioned clothing. One of the men smoked a clay pipe, and all of them wore long, bushy sideburns. Close by them, on Wood Street, stood an old hansom cab. Several students making their way up Wood Street from various clubs, were intrigued by the sight of the hansom cab and the quaint looking men leaning on the pillars, and surmised that, once again, Liverpool's streets were being used as the backdrop to some filmed period drama.

However, when one of the students gazed back at the men and the archaic horse-drawn vehicle, just moments after passing them, he was staggered to find that the outdated loafers and the hansom cab had vanished into thin air.

In the autumn of 2003, there was an exact repetition of this spooky incident. Once again, it was a group of students returning from the clubs who came upon the men and the hansom cab, and once again the ghosts and the cab vanished into the night air when one of them glanced back down Wood Street.

Of course, when the music hall was still in existence, the upper class concert-goers would leave through the rear entrance, where a waiting hansom cab, or four-wheeled growler, would be waiting to whisk them back to their palatial homes. Perhaps the men leaning on the pillars were the ghosts of these cabmen, waiting to take the toffs home.

Dominating the junction of Bold Street and Concert Street is 'Reconciliation' – a thirteen-foot-high cast iron sculpture by Stephen Broadbent, unveiled in September 1990. On the day the statue was unveiled, two other identical sculptures were unveiled simultaneously in Belfast and Glasgow, as a symbolic way of uniting the three cities.

RECONCILIATION
FROM HAUNTED LIVERPOOL 1 PAGE 87

One January, in the early 1990s, Angela, a nineteen-year-old Liverpool waitress, met Duncan, a twenty-year-old Glaswegian, at a Bold Street café. The couple immediately hit it off and after only one meeting felt as if they had known each other all their lives. And so, on 29 February Angela proposed to Duncan. It was a leap year and the traditional day upon which women can propose to their lovers. Duncan laughed at Angela's forwardness and agreed to marry her, but, as he had hardly any money coming in from his job, said that she would have to wait a while for her engagement ring.

Shortly afterwards, Duncan received a letter from his brother in Glasgow saying that his mother was seriously ill. The doctors had diagnosed a brain tumour but did not yet know whether it was cancerous or benign. Duncan decided that he would have to go back to Glasgow for a few days to see his mother, but Angela was unable to accompany him because she needed the money from her job to pay the bills. The couple enjoyed one more night out before Duncan set off for Scotland. They went to a club, and as they walked home, they started to kiss passionately, ending up embracing beneath the enormous iron statue in Concert Street. By coincidence the statue was also of two people embracing each other. Angela told Duncan to come back to Liverpool as soon as possible and started to cry. Duncan brushed away her tears, said he would miss her badly and that she would be on his mind all the time.

The next day Duncan left the city for his hometown. As she worked in the café, Angela kept thinking about her boyfriend and the things they had said to one another. She desperately longed for a letter or phonecall from him.

A whole week went by and he still had not been in touch. Angela, deeply concerned, went to the Central Library and scoured the Glasgow phone book, looking for Duncan's surname and address. She telephoned immediately and Duncan's brother Alastair answered and seemed very evasive about his brother's whereabouts. In the end he admitted that Duncan was depressed about his mother's condition and had drowned his sorrows in a local pub with a former girlfriend.

In a state of numbness and shock, Angela said, "Well tell him to get in touch with me as soon as possible, please," and she walked all the way from William Brown Street to the Dingle, with a choking lump in her throat. "How could he do this to me?" she kept on thinking. "He said he loved me."

Another week went by – the darkest week of her life. She could barely bring herself to eat and refused to go out with her friends. Each morning she would wait in vain for the postman to see if Duncan had sent a letter. Angela's two best friends, Gina and Zoe, finally persuaded her to go out with them. The girls went to a club in Wood Street and had a great night, during which Angela danced alongside her friends and managed to forget her troubles for a time.

At about 2.30 that morning the girls walked up Bold Street, singing and laughing – that is until they saw something that they would talk about for the rest of their lives – the ghostly figure of a young man was standing at the base of the statue in Concert Street. He had his back turned to the girls, so they could not see his face. His head was bowed and his hands were resting on the statue. The girls immediately halted in their tracks, because the figure was semi-transparent! Gina swore and started to run shouting, "It's a ghost! It's a ghost!"

Zoe and Angela grabbed her and told her to calm down. They were both more intrigued than frightened, but Angela almost fainted when the ghost turned round, because it was the ghost of Duncan. He slowly walked away from the statue and appeared to be crying.

Angela ran from her mates and clattered over in her high heels to the ghostly figure shouting, "Duncan! Duncan! It's me, Angela."

The ghost did not react, but just faded away into the night air.

The girls were so shocked and frightened that none of them could remember walking to Zoe's flat in Brownlow Hill. The three of them sat up all night, each of them going over and over their version of the perplexing incident.

A few days later, the flesh and blood Duncan walked into the café in Bold Street where Angela worked. She almost dropped the tray of cups and saucers she was carrying when she saw him standing there with a bunch of flowers. He explained that his mother had been operated on and that she was now well on the road to recovery, adding that the last few weeks had been a living nightmare. He strongly denied that he had been seeing his old flame – she had just provided platonic support for him in his hour of need, that was all.

Duncan then told her a very strange tale. He said that on the previous Friday, at 2.30am, he had been wandering the streets of Glasgow's city centre, when he saw an exact replica of the iron statue in Liverpool's Concert Street. He immediately thought of Angela and hugged the statue and kept picturing himself with the girl in Liverpool. At that exact moment, Angela and her friends had seen Duncan's doppelganger at the base of the same statue off Bold Street. Both Angela and Duncan had been completely unaware of the existence of the two other copies of the statue in Concert Street in Glasgow and Belfast, which makes this story even more incredible.

BOLD STREET

Now carry on up Bold Street until you get to Number 80, about half way up, and to a ladies fashion store and teashop, known as Jeff's of Bold Street, which is open from Monday to Saturday.

THE HAUNTED WISHING WELL

In the 1970s there were several sightings of an old woman who emerged out of the solid floor of the premises carrying a heavy bucket. A ghost investigator at the time suggested that her appearance was an indication that a well may have once existed in the basement of the shop, but a local historian said there were no records of a well in Bold Street.

However, when Jeff Pierce and some builders were renovating the basement of Number 80, they came across an old air-raid shelter which they had not realised was there before. During the removal of the shelter, the vestiges of a seventeenth century well were uncovered, and Jeff decided to rebuild this well, which can now be seen at his store. All coins thrown into the 'wishing well' are collected annually, and donated to the Alder Hey Rocking Horse Appeal.

Now go to Number 88 Bold Street. In 1966 this was the premises of a ladies outfitters and was the site of one of the most eerie paranormal encounters ever to take place in Liverpool.

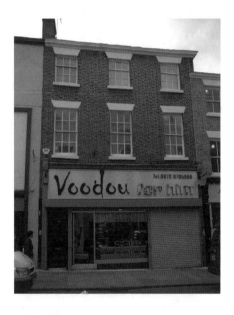

A MARRIAGE MADE IN HELL
FROM HAUNTED LIVERPOOL 3 PAGE 15

That year, a teenaged girl named Collette, was working at a factory in nearby Wood Street. Although she was pretty, she was a shy and introverted girl who had no real friends at the factory. She just kept herself to herself and hardly ever spoke to the eight other women who worked with her.

Each day at lunchtime, all the girls from the factory would go to a café in Bold Street, where they would laugh, giggle and gossip their way through lunch, but Collette never went with them. Instead she would go to a kiosk round the corner to buy cigarettes and would then walk up Bold Street, window shopping. She always seemed to be in a world of her own. Every day she would gaze longingly through the window of a certain shop which had expensive wedding dresses on display. She spent almost all of her lunch hour dreamily staring at these dresses. One of her workmates, Chrissy, remembers seeing Collette staring at the dresses and wondered what she was dreaming of.

Collette kept a diary of all her innermost thoughts, carefully recorded in her little black book. She used to fantasise about various film stars and wonder what type of man her future husband would be. She invariably imagined him to be tall, dark and handsome.

Collette was very attractive but seemed to have difficulty meeting members of the opposite sex. One night, at her flat in Huskisson Street, her old black neighbour Mona heard her sobbing. Mona did not want to interfere but the sobbing went on and on, so she tapped on Collette's door and asked if she was alright. Collette came to the door in a dreadful state – her eyes were red and swollen and she looked utterly forlorn. Mona took the girl down to her basement flat and gave her a cup of tea. Collette eventually revealed that she had plucked up courage and asked a boy out and he had turned her down. Mona tutted and shook her head and said the boy must have been a fool. She tried to boost the girl's confidence by saying she was very pretty and that boys were ten-a-penny.

About an hour later, as Collette left Mona's flat, she met a sinister old man on the stairs who had only just moved into the flats. She only knew him as Mr Rose and there was something very strange about him. He always dressed in black from head to toe and was invariably accompanied by a sleek, black cat with piercing green eyes.

"Hello, Mr Rose," Collette said, as she passed the old man on the stairs.

"If we meet on the stairs, we'll never meet in Heaven," he replied, referring to an old superstition. Then in a serious tone he told her, "Collette, I couldn't help overhearing you and Mona before."

"Yes?" said Collette defensively, starting to blush.

"I think I can help you. Come in," he said, beckoning her into his flat.

Collette felt very nervous as she entered the old man's dingy flat. The living room was littered with dusty old tomes on astrology and the occult and there was even a crystal ball on the table. The old man ushered her towards the table and handed her a piece of paper.

"That's a pact with the Devil," he explained in a matter-of-fact way and offered her a pen.

Collette grinned and looked at the words scrawled on the paper. They seemed to be in Latin and were so small, she could not make head nor tail of them.

"What does it say?" she asked.

"In return for your soul, you can have anything you desire. Just write your name at the bottom of the page," said Mr Rose and he uncapped an old fountain pen and handed it to the girl.

"I don't believe in all that stuff. There is no Devil," said Collette.

"I know, yes," said Mr Rose, growing agitated, "but just sign it anyway, go on."

"But ... but ..." stammered the girl.

"No buts. Just do it! Do it! Go on, you know you want to," said the old man, hypnotically staring at her.

Collette signed it and laughed.

"I want to marry a man who's tall, dark and handsome," she wished out loud, then left the room, giggling as she trotted up to her flat.

On the following day, during her lunch break, Collette was gazing into the window of the shop again, all her attention focused on the beautiful satin and lace wedding gown, when suddenly, she saw a face reflected in the window. It was the handsome face of a tall, dark-haired man. He was looking over her shoulder and his sudden presence startled her.

"Oooh! Who are you?" exclaimed Collette, blushing as she always did when she was talking to a man.

As she looked at the man he grinned broadly, which accentuated his handsome features. He looked so dashing yet there was something slightly menacing about him, then the pupils of his eyes suddenly burned with a dim red light.

Collette stumbled backwards against the window in fear. The figure then glided towards her without seeming to take any steps.

"Don't be afraid, Collette. I want to marry you. I want you. You made your promise to me," said the weird stranger, "and now I want you."

Collette let out a strangled scream and fled up Bold Street in a state of utter terror. Instead of going back to finish her afternoon shift at work, she ran home, barricaded herself inside her flat and hid under the table, her heart pounding.

At eight o'clock that night, the sinister stranger called at her flat in

Huskisson Street, just as she had feared he would. She looked out of her window and saw him standing in front of the door carrying a brown paper parcel. She screamed, "Don't let him in," but the old woman, Mona, had already opened the front door and allowed him to enter. He tapped on Collette's door, saying, "Let me in, Collette. I love you. I'm your future husband." Then his voice suddenly turned nasty and he began to shout. "Let me in, damn you!"

Then there was silence.

Collette sat up all night drinking coffee and listening to her radio. The visit had left her a nervous wreck. As soon as morning came she planned to leave her flat for good and she began writing down all the strange events that had happened in her diary, trying to make sense of them. However, Collette never managed to finish her entry for that day because she dropped dead from a massive heart attack, whilst still clutching her pen.

Mona went to check on Collette the next day and found her lifeless body. Her eyes were wide open, filled with terror.

When the police called at the flat to investigate the events surrounding her death, they found a brown paper parcel on the landing outside the girl's door. The contents of the parcel were the source of much speculation, for inside the package was a beautiful black silk and lace wedding dress, identical to the one in the shop in Bold Street, in everything but its colour.

When Mona read the dead girl's diary she shuddered and decided to confront Mr Rose, the man who, according to the diary, had persuaded Collette to sign the pact with the Devil. But Mr Rose's flat was deserted – not one of his fusty old books remained. Nobody had seen him leave and nobody ever set eyes on the old man again.

Now cross over to Number 89 Bold Street. This was once the address of the Odd Spot Club, which opened in 1961. In 1962, The Beatles played there, as did many other famous groups throughout the 1960s.

THE ODD SPOT

THE ODD SPOT Presents THE BEATLES
ALSO: "THE MERSEY BEATS"   29th MARCH   ADMISSION 6/- NEW MEMBERS WELCOME

In the late 1990s, over a period of about five months, a shop on Bold Street received numerous telephone calls on a regular basis from a man wanting to talk to the manager of the Odd Spot – which had closed down decades before. Engineers were called in to trace the persistent nuisance caller, and they were perplexed to discover that he could not be traced. A ghost investigator was brought in and confronted the caller on the telephone and asked if he was a ghost. After a long pause, the eerie caller hung up and never rang again.

ST LUKE'S CHURCH

Cross Berry Street and walk up Leece Street, staying on the right-hand side of the street until you come to the gates of St Luke's Church.

St Luke's Church was designed by John Foster (1759-1827), the dock engineer responsible for many grand public buildings which still stand in Liverpool today. Work began on the church in April 1811, and it was consecrated in January 1831. On the Monday night of 5 May 1941, St Luke's Church received a direct hit by a German incendiary bomb which completely gutted its interior, and the place of worship was left a hollowed-out ruin. It was decided to leave what remained of the church exactly as it was, as a lasting memorial to the terrible May Blitz which had devastated the city.

The grounds surrounding the church are now public gardens, and a memorial stone to the Irish Famine stands near the entrance gates in Leece Street. The place is simply alive with ghostly atmosphere and it comes as no surprise that it has been the scene of numerous other-worldly happenings over the years.

Walk through the Leece Street entrance to St Luke's and continue straight down the path until you come to the walled-up former arched entrance to the church. Turn left and walk round to the back of the church, which looks on to Bold Place. A very strange supernatural event took place here in December 1991 which has still never been fully explained.

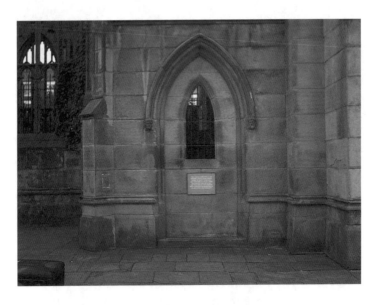

ABDUCTION AT ST LUKE'S

It all started one foggy Friday evening just before Christmas in 1991. It was 7pm and the Edwards family, of Dovecot, had decided to go and do a bit of late Christmas shopping in Liverpool city centre. Mr Edwards drove his wife and four children to town in his old Volvo estate and, as usual, finding a place to park proved to be very difficult. He drove around, searching desperately for a parking space, as his three sons and daughter gazed excitedly at the sparkling Christmas lights and decorations lining the streets. The youngest of the Edwards children was six-year-old Abbi. Like all six-year-olds she loved Christmas and for days she had been pestering her mum and dad to take her to see the enormous fir tree, covered with coloured lights, in Church Street.

As Abbi's dad was grumbling about finding a place to park the Volvo, her Mum suddenly pointed to a secluded side-street called Bold Place, which runs from Berry Street, past the back of St Luke's Church and up to Roscoe Street. Mr Edwards sighed with relief and turned left into the poorly-lit cobbled road, which was on a bit of an incline. As soon as the car was parked, the four children eagerly jumped out of the vehicle and started pestering their parents about what they were hoping to get for Christmas. Meanwhile, a strange icy fog bubbled up from nowhere and rolled down the street.

After checking that the doors of the car were locked, the two adults had a quick discussion about where they were going first. Mr Edwards wanted to go to a shop in Bold Street, to buy his father a cardigan, but his wife insisted on going to Dixons first, to buy a CD player for her sister. The children then started arguing too; naturally, their first priority was to visit the various toy stores. Their father's temper finally snapped.

"Alright, that's enough, will you all just shut up!"

The whole family immediately responded to the stress in his voice and quietened down, ready to set off. Suddenly, Mr Edwards noticed that one of the children was missing – and his heart skipped a beat. With a look of dread, he glanced frantically about Bold Place and yelled, "Where's Abbi?"

Everyone joined in the search for the lost child, firstly looking through the windows of the car, but finding no one there.

"Where on earth has she gone?" her mother pleaded, with a trembling voice. "She was here a minute ago."

The three boys looked desperately about, but the street was totally empty, with no sign of the missing child, or any other living soul.

At this point, they all heard a faint voice screaming out in the distance. "Daddy! Daddy!"

The voice definitely sounded like Abbi's and it came from the top of Bold Place, towards Roscoe Street. The family rushed up the cobbled road with Mr Edwards leading the way.

"Abbi! Abbi!" he called. "Where are you, Abbi? Don't play games now. Where are you hiding?"

The gates at the back of St Luke's were open and he surmised that his daughter must have wandered into the precincts of the old church. He hurried into the grounds, followed closely by his wife and their sons, and, once again, they could all hear Abbi crying out for her father. But the little girl was nowhere to be seen and the fog was getting thicker by the minute.

Mr Edwards was reluctant to alarm his wife and children, but he secretly wondered if some perverted lunatic had grabbed his daughter and taken her into the ruins of the old church. He handed his wife the car keys and asked her to go and bring the torch from the vehicle. When she returned, he climbed up on to the ledge of a church window and shone the flashlight into the shadowy ruins. The interior was completely deserted; deathly quiet with nothing but rubble scattered about. He knew that the church of St Luke had been gutted by an incendiary bomb during the Second World War during the May Blitz. Only the shell of the building had survived and the church had been deliberately left that way, as a reminder of the War. And yet it sounded as if Abbi's voice had come from inside the church.

As Mrs Edwards helped her husband down from the window, she put her fingers to her lips, "Listen!" she whispered. The faint eerie sound of a church organ was just audible and it too seemed to be coming from inside the church.

"Sound can play funny tricks at night," replied her husband dismissively. "Come on, let's go and get the police. This has gone beyond a joke." When his wife began to cry, he tried to reassure her. "It'll be alright. We'll find her, love, of course we will. She can't have gone far."

The distraught family set off for the police station in Hope Street and reported their lost daughter to the desk sergeant, who alerted all the patrol cars in the area and told officers on the city centre beat to be on the lookout for the girl. The family then rushed back to Bold Place to resume their search for the missing girl. They scoured the grounds of St Luke's once again and, after twenty minutes, they were about to return to their car, when something happened which continues to puzzle them to this day. A tall man, wearing a top hat and a long black coat, came out of the grounds of St Luke's and walking with him was little Abbi, holding his hand.

When Abbi caught sight of her mum and dad, she ran straight over to them and started to cry as her father picked her up. The sinister man in black looked like some stern figure out of the Victorian age. He had long bushy sideburns, a pallid face and penetrating, ink-black eyes. He stood like a statue outside the gates of the church and, in a creepy low voice, addressed them.

"Please accept my sincere apologies for any distress caused."

He then turned on his heels and walked silently back towards the rear of the church ruins.

Mrs Edwards grabbed Abbi from her husband.

"Are you all right, love? Where've you been?" she asked her frantically.

"I'm fine, Mummy."

Mr Edwards was furious and he shouted after the man:

"Oi! Who are you? What's your game, eh?"

Then a police patrol car came tearing down the road and he told the officers about the stranger who had appeared out of nowhere and returned his daughter. Three of them bolted from the car and rushed into the grounds of the church, wielding their batons, determined to catch the child abductor before he left the area.

But the police found no one. The grounds were completely empty. Police reinforcements turned up and the grounds were searched repeatedly with powerful torches, but the place was completely deserted. However, several police officers also heard the faint strains of a church organ playing somewhere nearby, but they were unable to determine exactly where the ethereal music was coming from.

One of the policemen asked little Abbi where she had been and the child gave a very strange account. She claimed that an old woman in a shawl had grabbed her hand and dragged her into the church, where a mass was being celebrated. Inside the church the whole congregation was dressed in old-fashioned clothing. The women wore big hats and the men were all dressed in black. Abbi had screamed for her father, but the old woman had put her hand over her mouth to silence her. Some time later, a tall man entered the church and pulled Abbi from the old woman's clutches. He had been the man who had delivered Abbi back to her parents.

The intrigued policeman continued to interrogate the child and he asked her if the man had spoken to her about the strange incident. Abbi shook her head, then added that he had said that he had been a long time dead. Everyone went quiet when they heard the child's strange reply and exchanged nervous glances.

Since the disturbing incident, the Edwards family have refused to go anywhere near St Luke's Church, especially during the Christmas period.

After recounting this unusual story on the radio, I received a lot of letters, phone-calls and e-mails, from people who also had weird tales to tell about St Luke's Church. A man who worked in Rapid Hardware in Renshaw Street told me how he had been driving to work early one morning, when he saw St Luke's lit up on the inside by quaint-looking chandeliers. He could even see stained glass windows and decided that the church must have been renovated. However, when the witness glanced at the traffic lights, out of the corner of his left eye, he watched the illumination from St Luke's start to fade. He turned to look back at the old church and noticed that the windows had now disappeared and the place was in total darkness once again. This was just one of the many accounts I have received regarding this beautiful church, which now provides a quiet oasis in the middle of the city.

A woman who worked in the Leece Street Job Centre, up until the 1980s, recently told me that during her lunch breaks, she would often cross the road and enjoy a sandwich or a cigarette in the quiet grounds of St Luke's Church. On many occasions, this woman, and several other people present, distinctly heard the faint hum of a church organ's bourdon note, the drone bass which always precedes a piece of organ music. The distinctive sound would drift and reverberate around the shell of the empty church. I even received an alleged tape recording of this music from a man living in Roscoe Street who said that he too often heard the music. It certainly did sound quite eerie and was later identified as an arrangement of Angels from the Realms of Glory, written in 1816.

RODNEY STREET (LEFT-HAND SIDE)

Leave St Luke's churchyard via the Leece Street gateway, and turn right up the street until you come to Rodney Street. Turn right into Rodney Street and immediately you will reach the first house, Number 34, situated on the corner of Rodney Street and Leece Street.

CAMERA OF PAST EVENTS

In Victorian times, Number 34 Rodney Street was the Tumour Hospital, where a number of strange incidents took place. Between 1887 and 1889, there were strange sightings of a very unusual and alarming apparition – that of a giant white cat, which was said to measure over five feet in height in a sitting position! This cat was reported by many seriously ill patients at the hospital, and was always seen in the sitting position at the foot of certain patients' sickbeds. Those who were lucky enough to see the blue-eyed phantasm usually experienced an inexplicable spontaneous return to full health. Of course, the cat was explained away by surgeons and doctors as a hallucination of a fevered mind, as was a smiling lady in white, who was also reported by the dying at the hospital on many occasions.

Now cross to Number 43 Rodney Street. In 1897, this was the address of Esme Collings Photographers, and in that year, a William Maplebeck and Robert Stookes, presented for public scrutiny a very controversial invention which they called a 'Chronoscope' – a camera that could take take pictures from the near and distant past. The camera used an arrangement of mirrored quartz lenses and various 'refracting mechanisms' to allegedly project images from long-vanished scenes on to film, or photographic plate. The device sounds like an early Fabry-Perot interferometer. If you hold a flat hand mirror towards a wall mirror you will see a tunnel of mirrors in the reflection that appears to go on to infinity, and this effect was at the heart of the 'Camera of Past Events', as it was known, or, more frequently, derided.

A gathering of the local Victorian intelligentsia was not impressed by the exhibition of the camera, and accused Maplebeck and Stookes of charlatanism. Public disapproval forced the two inventors to flee from Number 43, and the Chronoscope was virtually forgotten until talk of a Camera of Past Events started to circulate in California, and captured the cinematic imagination of Cecil B de Mille, the legendary Hollywood film director. He was contacted by an English inventor named Baird T Spalding and a scientist (and friend of Einstein) named Charles Steinmetz. The two men claimed they could construct such a camera, and were financed by de Mille and sent to the Middle East with the invention, to hopefully capture images of Jesus and the Hebrew Prophets. Then Spalding suddenly vanished from public sight, and there were rumours that the authorities had purchased the patent for the camera. With such a camera, the world of forensic science would be revolutionised, for we could aim it at the scene of a murder and capture the killer on video! There are rumours that one Chronoscope is still hidden away in a vault beneath the Vatican.

Cross back over the road to two more interesting addresses in this street.

PHANTOM STALKERS

Number 72 Rodney Street was the surgery of William J Callon, MD and surgeon, who also had an interest in illnesses of the human mind. This was in the days before Freud and psychoanalysis and complexes, of course, yet Callon did suspect the existence of the subconscious and a 'super-conscious'. Callon was also intrigued by instances of telepathy. One day he received a request to see a patient from London, referred to him by a colleague, Dr R Williams. The patient, a Mr Runcy, seemed to be suffering from supernatural persecution. Runcy came from Liverpool originally but had moved to London after inheriting a vast fortune.

The notes of Dr Williams, published in a psychiatric journal in the 1920s, detail the history of this wealthy, thirty-three-year-old Liverpool man.

In 1899, Runcy was living in the Knightsbridge area of London. Having become extremely wealthy overnight, he was therefore in the fortunate position of not having to work to support himself. One morning, in July 1899, he awoke with a fearful hangover after a night of hard-drinking with his equally wealthy and dissolute companions. As Runcy sat up in bed, rubbing his throbbing head and squinting at the bright sunlight filtering through the curtains, he noticed a strange black cat sitting on the carpet facing him. Its piercing eyes seemed to be of an almost luminous cobalt blue, and it sat staring intently at the man of leisure as he struggled to make sense of its sudden appearance. Runcy was baffled. He did not own a cat – he didn't particularly like animals – and so he surmised that one of his madcap friends had put the creature in the house as some kind of childish prank.

However, Runcy soon came to realise that the cat was no ordinary animal, as he was the only one who could actually see it; the maids, butlers, servants and cooks could not see any black cat, with or without glowing blue eyes, and neither could Runcy's friends.

Wherever Runcy went, the cat went too. He strolled through Hyde Park to try and rid himself of his hangover, and so did the hallucinatory cat. He visited a friend's home in Belgravia, and there was the cat, curled up on the rug, not taking his eyes off his quarry for a moment. Runcy tried to tell himself that the cat did not exist, that it was all some strange figment of his imagination, possibly brought about by the heavy drinking sessions in which he had been indulging, but all the same, the dreaded slinky black phantasm stalked him incessantly, until he was convinced that he was going insane.

Runcy eventually confided in a close friend about the irksome feline vision, and this friend referred him to Dr Williams, whose West End practice specialised in psychiatric illnesses. Dr Williams ordered Runcy to cease his life of debauchery at once. The all-night parties, the absinthe sprees, the outsized cigars, the rich, exotic food and the womanising were to be replaced by a month of total rest and abstinence. Runcy was ordered to eat simple, bland food and to be in bed by no later than ten o'clock every night.

So worried was the young libertine, that he followed the doctor's orders to the letter and, in doing so, incurred the ridicule of his hellfire friends. However, within a week, the black cat had vanished and Runcy was so relieved that he went to thank Dr Williams in person, after which he whistled his way back home to Knightsbridge with a new spring in his step, mentally planning the night out he was going to enjoy. The cat was gone, so he had no need to stick to Williams' strict routine any more.

However, his new-found peace of mind was to be short-lived, because as he was walking up the long hallway towards the stairs – a strange-looking man in eighteenth century clothing greeted him. The man wore a small white wig with a ribbon bow tied to its pigtail, and a long crimson satin coat embroidered with an intricate floral design. His black velvet trousers went down as far as the knees, and below that he wore white stockings and a pair of shiny, square-buckled shoes. This outlandish figure beckoned the dumbstruck Runcy with a small sword, which he waved towards the stairs.

"Who the devil are you?" Runcy asked the stranger, but the stranger said nothing, and only smiled in reply.

Runcy soon discovered that the bizarre character – like the black cat – could not be perceived by anyone else, and like the cat, this apparition followed him about everywhere. When he retired to bed at night, Runcy would peep over his blankets and catch sight of the old-fashioned phantom standing to attention in the form of a silhouette against the curtains. In the morning, the figure would still be standing in the same position, waiting for Runcy to rise, ready to resume shadowing him wherever he should go.

Dr Williams was most concerned by the new 'ideoform' as he called it, and he arranged for Runcy to be hypnotised in order to expunge the vision from his mind, but even hypnosis could not cancel out the imaginary tormentor. Little did Runcy or Williams know that the hallucinatory nuisance would soon be replaced by a truly terrifying apparition.

One Sunday evening, Runcy was walking quickly along Portland Place in the rain, desperately trying to shake off the eighteenth century stalker who accompanied him everywhere. These days, Runcy routinely glanced behind him every few yards in the hope that he would find the phantom gone. He was invariably disappointed but on this occasion he noted with great relief that the street was deserted. There was no sign of the man from his imagination. He rushed homeward, constantly looking over his shoulder and checking the road ahead, but the annoying follower was still nowhere to be seen.

Runcy then enjoyed three days entirely free of the man in the white wig and was just beginning to feel himself again, when, on the fourth day, his new-found composure was completely shattered. He had ventured out to a theatre in Covent Garden, and his companion was a beautiful woman named Lydia Ellen, a young lady who had many admirers. Runcy was paying little attention to the play, being otherwise occupied whispering sweet nothings into the lovely Lydia's ear, when something suddenly caught his eye. Standing in the central aisle of the theatre, close to the end seat of Runcy's row, stood a tall human skeleton. Runcy stared in horror at the latest apparition born of his troubled mind. Lydia immediately noticed the look of horror on his face, and followed the line of his gaze to the central aisle – and saw nothing amiss. The skeleton's gleaming white head slowly turned and faced Runcy; its black eye sockets seemed to penetrate his own and its teeth and jaw were set in the frozen grin typical of a human skull.

Runcy was so distracted by the creepy skeleton that Lydia soon became irritated. She was convinced that her beau was eyeing some other lady in the auditorium. She was used to being the sole centre of attention and in the end, with a rustle of silk petticoats, she stormed out of the theatre in a huff. The skeletal creature of Runcy's psyche had completely ruined his evening.

Runcy jumped into a hansom cab outside the theatre – and so did the skeleton; its bones rattling horribly whenever it made the slightest movement. He dashed into his home ahead of the skeleton, and slammed the front door. He then breathlessly ordered a puzzled servant to bolt all the doors and windows in the house, but when Runcy reached the drawing room, he saw, to his horror, that the skeleton was already there, warming itself in front of the blazing fire, with its fleshless bony hands clasped behind its curving spine.

After years of persecution from the skeletal stalker, Runcy visited Dr William Callon at Number 72 Rodney Street, at the suggestion of Dr Williams – and the skeleton came with him, of course. Doctor Callon examined his patient thoroughly and asked him where the skeleton was standing at that moment.

"Next to your desk, sir," was Runcy's reply.

When Callon stood in the space where the skeleton was supposed to be, he felt a sharp chill which penetrated the whole of his body. Callon, like Williams, called the hallucination an 'ideoform', but despite prescribing opiate-based drugs, the skeleton remained loyally attached to the young man. Wherever Runcy went, the rattling skeleton followed, and even when Dr Callon suggested a trip abroad, the grotesque figure took the advice too. It stuck like glue to Runcy during his entire stay in Switzerland, stalking him up the highest mountains and across the deepest lakes.

Unfortunately, there is no happy ending to this tale.

After almost a decade of non-stop persecution, Runcy ended up in a lunatic asylum, and it is said that he died in Bedlam. Even upon his deathbed, he could still see the grinning face of the skeleton, peering between the faces of his family as they attended him in his final hours.

Were the cat, the old-fashioned gentleman and the skeleton all figments of a mind beset with severe mental illness, or did the persecuting entities have an independent existence of their own?

Stay on the same side of Rodney Street, and turn right into Knight Street, then go down to Number 43. Two very strange disappearances took place at this house.

CONGO CONUNDRUM

In 1878, Sarah Harvey, an eighteen-year-old Liverpool woman, went missing from her Knight Street home.

One evening she went up to her bedroom to prepare herself for an evening out at the theatre with her young man, full of pleasant expectation. They were going to see a play at the Colosseum Theatre in Paradise Street and she was very excited by the prospect. When her young escort arrived to collect her, the girl's mother sat him down in the front parlour and trotted upstairs to fetch her daughter. She knocked on the bedroom door but there was no answer, so she opened the door and stepped inside. Sarah was nowhere to be found. There was nothing unusual about the room, a few clothes were strewn about

40

and various other articles such as combs, hairpins and ribbons were just where her daughter had left them on her dressing table, but there was no sign of Sarah.

Then Mrs Harvey noticed an upturned wine glass on the dresser and wondered who had could have put it there and why it was upside down. This part of the puzzle was solved the next day when Sarah's friend told her mother that they had been playing with a ouija board a few evenings before. Despite the most thorough investigation, there were no other clues as to her disappearance and, to the great distress of her family, Sarah Harvey was never found.

Ten years later, a British team of explorers in equatorial Africa came across a remote tribe of pygmies. The tribe's witchdoctor, a wizened old man with skin like tanned leather, was stretched out in one of the huts, dying. The explorers offered him some of their western medicine, but he refused. Shortly before he died, he made a startling confession through an interpreter. Although his breathing was becoming very laboured, it was obvious that he was determined to reveal what was on his mind.

Beckoning the explorers towards him, he whispered his confession. He claimed that, some years earlier, he had spirited away a golden-haired woman from a faraway island to his hut deep in the rainforest. Incredibly, he told them that her name was Sarah Harvey. The witchdoctor went on to say that one night she had escaped from the hut and run away from him whilst he was sleeping and that a grey-haired Sarah Harvey was last reported to be living with another African tribe deep in the Congo.

Can this far-fetched tale possibly be true? Did the witchdoctor really teleport Miss Harvey from her cosy bedroom in a respectable Liverpool street, to a mud hut in the middle of the dark continent? If not, how did he come by her name? and what *did* happen to Sarah Harvey? Had her dabblings with the ouija board some connection with her disappearance?

BABY SNATCH

By a very strange coincidence, in the 1880s, a young female baby of ten months vanished from her nursery at the same house. The baby's guardian, Robina Tillotson, noticed that the baby's cradle was rocking quite violently, thinking that the baby had awakened and was in some kind of distress, she went to pick up the child, but she wasn't in the cradle. Several policemen descended on the household to investigate the baffling child-snatching incident and quizzed everyone staying there, including a shoemaker by the name of Stephen Owen. Owen was only too eager to talk to the policemen and told them that the place was haunted. Seconds later, the detectives and the shoemaker heard a woman's voice close by announce: "We have returned her."

Then came the sound of a baby crying upstairs. The policemen and virtually the entire household dashed upstairs to find that the child had been returned to its cradle, and was now swathed in strange burgundy and saffron cloth. At the time of the baby's reappearance, a constable had been standing on guard outside the nursery door, and had seen no one enter the room.

Other strange goings on were reported at the house. That same night, a woman singing in a high, operatic voice was heard on the upper floors of Number 43, and days later, a tailor named Gill, who was lodging at the house, said an invisible hand had stroked his head while he was sitting in his armchair.

Go back up to the top of Knight Street and turn right back into Rodney Street. Halfway along this row of Georgian terraced houses you will find the impressive double doors of Number 78 – the scene of another disturbing tale.

A DANGEROUS EXPERIMENT
FROM HAUNTED LIVERPOOL 8

This story concerns the misuse of a drug for selfish gain; the over-indulgence in a dangerous mind-expanding drink that caused two egotistical but innocent men to become gibbering idiots.

At Number 78 Rodney Street, Liverpool's equivalent of Harley Street, was the prestigious practice of George Arthur Williams, a Harvard-educated dental surgeon. He was a man who also had a wide knowledge of anaesthesia. Williams had a cousin in Mexico who collected various plants with medicinal properties and dispatched them to him and Williams wrote several tracts on the coca plant from which the drug cocaine is derived. In 1886, John Pemberton had introduced the popular drink Coca-Cola to consumers in America. Amongst other ingredients, the drink contained cocaine, syrup and caffeine. In 1901, the cocaine was removed from the soft drink, because it was thought to be addiction-forming.

As far back as 3000 BC, coca chewing was practised throughout South America to stave off hunger and give extra energy, and the plant was regarded as a gift from God. The Incas cultivated large coca plantations that were later taken over by the Spanish invaders.

George Arthur Williams researched other less-known plants of medicinal value, such as the peyote cactus, which contains a chemical that somehow transforms sounds entering the ear into a kaleidoscope of colours in the brain. Williams experimented with the cactus extract, but found it was of little use in the annulment of pain from tooth nerves. Williams also dabbled with huanta, a toxic plant from Ecuador with white blossoms, which has the reputation of being the main ingredient in the so-called 'Sorcerer's Drink' which caused shamans to fall into a coma for three days at a time, until they awakened imbued with supernatural wisdom. When Williams drank the diluted juice of the plant, he ended up with nothing more than a lingering headache.

However, the one plant that did seem to hold great potential for the creation of a new pain-killing compound, was a tropical American vine called Yage (pronounced ya-hay). This plant had acquired something of a legendary status in Europe, but obtaining it was exceedingly difficult, as it was mainly found in Amazonia. Williams received a parcel one morning from his cousin across the Atlantic. It was a coil of Yage vine measuring just thirty-six inches in length, sent from Belem in South America. Williams took down a huge, leather-bound volume on the exotic flora of the South American Continent and flipped through the pages until he came upon the section that documented the yage plant and its use in various controversial preparations.

In order to extract the vital ingredient of the plant, a portion of the vine was to be boiled in distilled water for fourteen hours until it was reduced to a residue. The residue had to be further treated until its essence had been isolated. This distilled spirit then had to be rediluted by infusing it into wine made from the noha grape. The noha grape was banned in France in the 1970s by the French Ministry of Agriculture because the wine it produces is thought to cause insanity through the release of a chemical similar to an hallucinogen found in marijuana.

After several months, Williams managed to produce two bottles of the Yage wine and he stored it in the cellars of 78 Rodney Street. Meanwhile, he devoured as much information on yage as possible, and even travelled to the reading rooms of the British Library in London to read up on the plant, which was classified under the Latin name of banisteriopsis caapi. Williams read various accounts of the effects which yage wine had on a person once it had been imbibed. Most people who had drunk the wine afterwards told how they had been confronted by terrifying, realistic monsters which did not seem to be yage-induced hallucinations at all. Had they been drug-induced figments of the mind, the appearance and behaviour of the horrifying phantasms should have varied from person to person, but this was not the case. The people who perceived the monsters always described them in exactly the same way.

There were three species of these monsters: grotesque, gargoyle-like beings; globular black octopuses with squirming tentacles; and an enormous black cat, reminiscent of a panther. The Ecuadorian shamans maintained that these creatures could only be repelled by strong willpower. A weak-minded person would be attacked by the entities, and would either die, or return to the real world with an insane mind. Once the creatures had been 'tamed', the person who had absorbed the yage wine would be capable of receiving a 'cosmic wisdom' and of even communicating with the dead. The most hazardous part of the entire experiment hinged on consuming exactly the right quantity of wine. Too much, and it would almost certainly result in incurable madness.

George Arthur Williams wrestled with the pros and cons of personally experimenting with the dangerous brew, and many times he took one of the unlabelled dark purple bottles of yage wine from the cool cellar and gazed at it. He would repeatedly touch the cork and feel an almost overpowering urge to reach for the corkscrew. But he wasn't quite ready yet. What if the stories of the monsters from another reality were true?

At a gentlemen's club in Liverpool in May 1906, Williams was smoking his pipe as he stared out of the window into the evening sky. He was contemplating the possibility of using a guinea pig upon which to test the potent wine, when two acquaintances approached him and disturbed his reverie. They were the tall, broad-shouldered Saxon Hill, a successful stockbroker from St Michael's-in-the-Hamlet, and his friend

Thomas Canning, a wealthy confectioner who had sold numerous cake recipe books to hotels across Europe. Williams talked to them about the dangerous wine, and the two men responded with sceptical smirks.

Saxon Hill bragged that he was immune to intoxication, and told a rambling story of how he had remained standing after a drinking spree that lasted twelve hours. Each of his other drinking companions finished up lying prostrate on the floor, and one drinker had almost died of alcohol poisoning.

Canning declared that he had never heard of Williams' yage wine, despite the fact that he was one of the greatest wine connoisseurs in England. Hill lit a huge, ostentatious Havana cigar and offered himself as the ideal guinea pig for the American dentist. Williams instantly took up his offer, but only on the condition that he would not be sued if the wine 'tilted' Hill's brain. Hill promised that he would get a solicitor to draw up a legal document that would exculpate Williams from any responsibility, should the wine incur any damage to his mental health. The stockbroker seemed excited at the possibility of trying the mystical wine, but Canning predicted that the proposed experiment would come to nothing. The confectioner said that he had once inhaled nitrous oxide in his youth because a medical student friend had sworn that the gas provided instant enlightenment. All it had done was make Canning giggle and feel as if he was caught between waking and sleeping.

On the evening of Monday 7 May 1906, Saxon Hill and Thomas Canning arrived together at 78 Rodney Street, and were admitted by a servant and shown into the drawing room, where a bottle of purple yage wine stood in the centre of a small mahogany table on a silver salver. Next to the bottle was a crystal wine glass and a corkscrew fashioned from a piece of horn. Williams entered the room, and a smiling Saxon Hill handed him the legal document which guaranteed that no action would be taken against him, should the experiment end tragically. As Williams perused the document, Canning drew Hill's attention to an upright wooden chair which was swathed in thick leather straps. Williams explained that Hill would be put in that chair and restrained for his own protection, in case he became violently hysterical as a reaction to the yage. Most people in their right minds would have fled on seeing the chair, but the indomitable Hill seemed to be relishing the drama of the situation.

Saxon Hill inserted the corkscrew into the bottle as Williams warned him to be very careful. Williams began to have serious doubts about the experiment, not for Hill's sake, but for his own reputation. If the wine produced no effect, the American would be ridiculed for ever more. He was still wondering whether it was wise to proceed, when, all of a sudden, he felt a sharp nagging pain in his abdomen. The pain was so severe it winded him and made him double up. He had suffered from the same stomach pains at breakfast, and he feared it might be the return of what the doctors had diagnosed as a grumbling appendicitis. The pain receded for a while, and Williams sat at the table, breathing deeply, with his hand over his navel. Saxon Hill poured the wine into a glass, held it up to the bright gas mantle, then sniffed it. "Smells quite sweet," he said.

"Just sip it, Mr Hill," cautioned Williams.

But the foolhardy Hill ostentatiously threw back his head and downed the entire glass in one gulp.

"No!" wailed Williams, all the time thinking about all the literature he had read which had warned about the precise dosage of the yage and noha grape concoction.

"I say, calm down, man," said Hill, licking his lips. "The drink hasn't been invented which can damage my iron constitution!"

Williams took out his fob watch and removed the cover to inspect the dial. The time was 7.35pm. According to all the literature he had read, yage took ten minutes to enter the bloodstream via the stomach wall.

As those ten minutes elapsed, Saxon Hill repeatedly pronounced that he felt as right as rain, and expressed disappointment with Williams who had promised such great things of the drink. At this point, having watched Hill down the wine with no obvious ill effects, Canning's curiosity got the better of him and he picked up the wine bottle, sniffed it's mouth, then took a small swig from it, even though Williams protested.

"It tastes rather plummy," was Canning's verdict, as he strode over to the window and gazed out at the gathering twilight.

Saxon Hill mentioned that he and his sweetheart Leonora would be travelling to New York on the White Star liner *Adriatic* on the following day, then, producing an expensive diamond ring from his waistcoat pocket, he told Canning how he planned to propose to her on deck in mid-Atlantic.

"You romantic fool, Saxon," laughed Canning, turning to find Saxon Hill trembling all over his body. He seemed to be having some kind of fit. His eyes bulged alarmingly, and he wore an expression of sheer terror on his contorted face.

Williams noted Saxon's behaviour with a mixture of dread and curiosity.

"Saxon, what on earth's the matter with you, dear fellow?" asked Canning, going to the aid of his friend, but as he walked around the table he suddenly felt an intense, burning pain in the middle of his forehead, which forced his eyes to close tightly. Canning held his head in his hands and let out a horrible scream.

Saxon Hill was still standing, albeit with an unnatural, rigid posture, despite the shuddering tremors which had gripped his body. He tried to utter something, but instead he began to foam at the mouth. His eyes seemed much whiter and larger than normal and threatened to bulge out of their sockets. The foam frothed and dribbled down Hill's beard and on to his waistcoat.

Canning, meanwhile, was now face-down on the hearthrug, convulsing uncontrollably, and yelping the words, "Stop! Stop! Stop!"

At this point, a maidservant who had heard the commotion, barged into the drawing room and witnessed the horrendous sight of the two men gripped by some kind of strange insanity. As the servant looked on, Saxon Hill stumbled backwards into a corner and shielded his eyes with the back of his hand. Then, with his bare hands, Thomas Canning started grabbing red hot pieces of coal from the fire and began hurling them at something only he could see on the floor.

Williams ordered the maid to fetch a doctor at once, and she closed the door and ran downstairs. She left the front door ajar and dashed across the road to the house of a Doctor Hamilton and informed him of the shocking scene she had just witnessed. When Hamilton and the maid entered the drawing room, they saw only Williams, initially, lying on the floor in obvious agony, clutching at his abdomen. Then the doctor and the maid heard the muffled sounds of someone crying. They traced the sobbing to Hill and Canning, who were cowering together under the table in abject terror.

Williams was taken to the Royal Infirmary on Pembroke Place, where an emergency appendectomy was carried out on him. He made a full recovery, and subsequently learned of the chilling fate of Saxon Hill and Thomas Canning who were not so lucky. Hill was being kept under lock and key in a room at the house of his brother, where he did nothing but tremble in a corner and mutter unintelligibly to himself. He had been certified insane and his family had been told that there was no hope of him being cured. His sweetheart Leonora had sailed to America without him, and after learning of his insanity, had deserted him. Those who listened to Hill's ramblings said that he spoke of a hideous black squid, with a single green eye, that continuously coiled its writhing tentacles about him.

Thomas Canning's insanity had rendered him a danger to himself as well as others, and he had been confined to a Lancashire lunatic asylum. He also told of being tormented by a repulsive tentacled creature that resembled a giant brown octopus, and of a long black panther, the size of a horse, which had glowing red eyes. Both creatures stalked him all day and all night. Canning felt so persecuted by the horrific creatures that he gouged out one of his own eyes in an attempt to blind himself. He later died in Bedlam lunatic asylum.

Saxon Hill never recovered and faded into obscurity.

Having destroyed the lives of two of his friends, not surprisingly, Williams abandoned his experiments with hallucinogens and stuck to dentistry as he had been taught it at university.

Drug researchers do not currently understand how yage affects perception, and the noha grape used in the wine mixture is still banned in most countries.

ST JAMES'S CEMETERY

Now walk across to the left side of Rodney Street, and continue along to the Duke Street end. Cross Duke Street at the traffic lights and walk towards one of the most magnificent cathedrals in the world – Liverpool's towering Anglican Cathedral, built using deep red sandstone, quarried locally in the village of Woolton, and standing on the ancient St James's Mount.

Go through the gateway to the sloped entrance path, down to St James's Cemetery, where over fifty thousand of the Victorian dead lie at rest – well most of them anyway … Almost fifty-eight thousand people are interred in the ten acres of ground which make up St James's Cemetery, a sunken churchyard in a former quarry. Go through the gates on Duke Street and down through the arched tunnel into this cemetery, and then take a sharp left. You will come to the ancient sandstone faces of St James's Mount, also known as Mount Zion in earlier times.

THE MOUNT

This site was revered by the pre-Christian cult that we now know as the Wiccans, and has a dark association with a legendary Lancashire witch named Jenna Green, who was cast out from her coven for some obscure reason – perhaps she misused her powers – although there are hints in a Liverpool nursery rhyme of yore that love and greed were the cause of the expulsion:

On the Mount there stands a lady,
Who she is I do not know,
All she wants is gold and silver,
All she wants is a very nice beau.

Look closely upon the sandstone faces of the mount and you will detect sinister etchings of devil's forks, strange glyphs, swastikas and the three-legged trident, which now symbolises the Isle of Man. The symbol was the coat of arms of the greatly feared Manx magician, Mannannan MacLlyr, who had a cloak of invisibility, the power to levitate and fly, and the lethal gift of killing at a distance through his potent magic. His gigantic tomb can still be seen at Peel Castle.

During excavations at St James's Mount in the late Edwardian period, workmen unearthed a curious-looking old statue of a long-haired woman with outstretched arms, wearing an ankle-length gown and what looked like a crown of laurel leaves upon her head. Around the circular plinth upon which this statue stood, there were inscriptions resembling Runic glyphs. Further digging around the statue revealed the vestiges of ancient dwellings, all arranged in a circle about the statue, as if some ancient community had revered the female figure. A drinking well was also found on the site but subsequently filled in, and the statue – which would have been of immense archaeological value – was taken away by one of the diggers to adorn his garden in Woolton. This statue was last seen in the 1950s and is now lost. Could it have been a graven idol of Jenna Green, known to later generations of Lancashire children as Ginny Greenteeth? Ginny was said to be an old witch who prowled the banks of streams and rivers, and a subterranean stream does indeed course beneath St James's cemetery until it emerges as a spring in the eastern wall. We will investigate this spring further on in this section of the walk.

Turn your attention to the gravestones near the wall, and in particular the polished granite headstone of Mary Allen, aged forty-six, and her fifteen-year-old son Ernest Allen. Mother and son both perished when the ship they were travelling on – the *SS Ellan Vannin* – sank in very mysterious circumstances.

For thousands of years, the belief has persisted that certain people and objects can bring misfortune. This story tells of a spectacular emerald-like gemstone which folklorists have nicknamed 'The Green Eye of the Mersey', which brought death and destruction to all those who were unfortunate enough to own it.

THE GREEN EYE OF THE MERSEY
FROM HAUNTED LIVERPOOL 3

On 21 October 1839, the night skies over Cheshire lit up with a blinding blue flash and scores of people witnessed the rare sight of a meteor falling to earth. The following morning, a farmer near Hollowmoor Heath discovered a small crater in his field. None of the cows would venture near the site of the meteoric impact and the farmer noticed that there was an unusual black object, the size of a billiard ball, embedded in the centre of the crater. The farmer showed the object to a clergyman and he passed it on to a friend, William Ibbotson, who was an amateur astronomer. Ibbotson cleaned the meteorite and sawed it in half. In the middle of the globe there was an object that was so hard, that the blade of the saw bounced off of it. Ibbotson realised that the object was a precious stone which was white, like an opal.

The unearthly gemstone was the size of an egg and had a peculiar flaw – it contained a circular emerald-coloured gemstone which made the stone resemble a glass eye with a green iris. Ibbotson despatched a report of his find to the Royal Astronomical Society in London but never received a reply. He decided that the 'Green Eye', as he called it, would be an unusual birthday gift for his niece who lived in Dublin.

Five months later, Ibbotson boarded the steamer *William Huskisson* at Liverpool Docks with the intention of delivering the stone to his Irish niece, but the ship never reached Ireland. It is not known why the steamship sank in the middle of the Irish Sea, since it was in excellent condition and its captain and crew had made the crossing hundreds of times before. Nevertheless, forty passengers, including Mr Ibbotson, perished beneath the waves.

Weeks later, Ibbotson's suitcase was washed up on the Wirral coast at Hoylake and a man named George Peters retrieved the case. When he opened it he discovered the strange Green Eye stone. After taking it to a jeweller who was unable to identify it, Peters decided to try and sell it in Liverpool. Alas, he was never able to carry out his plan because within twenty-four hours he was dead, the victim of a typhoid-like fever which claimed fifteen thousand other victims in the town. So-called 'Fever Sheds' were opened at Mount Pleasant and the body of William Peters was literally thrown on to a heap of corpses in one of these sheds.

A poor Irishman named John Lorne stripped and searched the plague corpses and came across the Green Eye. He was naturally delighted at his lucky find and showed it to his friends at a pub in Hope Street, telling them he intended to have it valued. The landlord of the pub was very superstitious and sensitive to all things paranormal. He thought the gemstone radiated evil and told Lorne to take it off the premises immediately. The Irishman laughed at the landlord's comments and set off home, whistling at his good fortune.

Half an hour later, a boy ran into the pub and cried that Lorne was dying outside his lodging house in Percy Street. Lorne was impaled on the railings in front of the house and was barely alive. Two railings had gone through his back and were protruding from his chest. He coughed up blood as he gave an account of what had happened. He said that a man had barged into his room and demanded the gemstone. There was a violent struggle as Lorne's assailant tried to prise the stone from his hands. In his frustration the man had pushed Lorne through his open window and he had landed on the railings. Lorne's friends made the fatal mistake of trying to lift their companion off the railings before medical help arrived, despite his agonising screams. Their well-meant intentions killed Lorne because, as they lifted him, one railing severed a major artery and the other ruptured his liver.

The Green Eye gemstone fell out of Lorne's hand and clattered on to the pavement. One of the bystanders picked up the stone and a fight broke out over who should have it. Eventually, the dead man's cousin, George Wishart, claimed it and he later emigrated to the Isle of Man.

One day, Wishart decided that he would go and have the Green Eye mounted in a gold locket, but on his way to the jewellers, he dropped dead in the street. A pathologist concluded that he had died from cardio-congestive failure but could not understand why, as Wishart had a cast-iron constitution.

Wishart's niece, a woman named May Allen, took possession of the jinxed gemstone and, within a year, five of her friends had died in tragic accidents. Even so, Mrs Allen refused to believe that the Green Eye was cursed.

In December 1909, she decided to visit relatives in Liverpool with her son Ernest. They both boarded a steamship called the SS *Ellan Vannin* and yes, you've guessed it, the ship sank in mysterious circumstances on its way into the port in Liverpool Bay. Look-outs in the Wirral lighthouse were horrified to see the *Ellan Vannin's* lights suddenly go out, followed, seconds later, by the ship sinking under the waves. All thirty-five passengers and crew on board the ship were drowned and the cause of the sudden sinking has never been determined, but a fourteen-foot hole of unknown origin was found on the portside of the ship's hull. The bodies of May and Ernest Allen were buried on the western side of St James's Cemetery, next to the Anglican Cathedral.

Relatives of Mrs Allen confirmed that she had definitely taken the Green Eye stone with her to show it to her cousins in Liverpool, but the gem was not found on her body. We must therefore presume that the cursed Green Eye gemstone is lying somewhere at the bottom of the Mersey, probably within the wreck of the *Ellan Vannin*, which still lies beneath the waves of Liverpool Bay.

Considering the dark and tragic history of all those who have owned it, perhaps the Green Eye of the Mersey should be left where it lies.

Walk from the western side of the cemetery, away from the Mount, and to the northern slopes, where you will come across a small wood. Since the 1920s there have been alleged sightings of the 'little people' here.

TARNEY'S WOOD

The most interesting encounter with one of these elusive beings took place here in June, 1932, when Susan Carmichael, aged thirteen, her younger brother David, aged eleven, and their little sister – six-year-old Lucy, met an elflike entity who called himself Tarney. The little man measured about three feet from the tip of his pointed green hat to his tiny boots, and was dressed in a brown, one-piece suit. His face looked quite old and wizened and his eyes had a particular golden tint, yet he spoke in a clear Lancashire accent.

Tarney came on the scene as Lucy, the youngest child, fell over whilst climbing up the slope into the wood. He helped the child up, and she smiled at him, but the two older children were naturally very apprehensive about the strangely dressed miniature person, who somehow knew their full names and many other details about their lives. The children – all from Bamber Bridge – were staying at their aunt's house on Hope Street for several weeks, and each day that summer they would hurry down to the cemetery to play with their newfound friend and to join in many adventures with the 'Ologs' and the 'Dwees' – two warring races of the little folk who live under the Mount in caverns and tunnels.

This is a very strange tale but surely that's all it is? A tale? Well, the story of Tarney was backed up from a few unusual and credible sources. A policeman who walked the Hope Street beat in the 1920s had been ridiculed when he told his wife that he had seen fairies playing about in St James's Cemetery after dark. Then, none other than Frederick William Dwelly, the First Dean of Liverpool, also expressed interest in the Tarney encounters, and said he had heard many tales of the little people being seen down in St James's Cemetery over the years, and had no reason to doubt the witnesses.

From Tarney's wood, continue walking to the north-eastern corner of the cemetery, and you will come upon the grave of one William Harrison, who was captain of Isambard Kingdom Brunel's gargantuan super-liner, the *Great Eastern*, his jinxed supership.

CAPTAIN OF THE CURSED SUPER-LINER
FROM HAUNTED LIVERPOOL 4

Mariners are renowned for their superstitions. To the seafarer, the sight of an albatross flying over a ship is a warning of an approaching storm and, as Coleridge recounted in *The Rime of the Ancient Mariner*, to kill such a bird would bring an eternity of bad luck. Without a doubt, the unluckiest ship that ever sailed was built at the yards of John Scott Russell in Milwall, London, over a period of three years in the late 1850s. The *Great Eastern* was the brainchild of one of the greatest engineers of all time; Isambard Kingdom Brunel. At nineteen thousand tons, the gigantic vessel was the most ambitious engineering project of the nineteenth century. The colossal six hundred and ninety-two-foot long, iron-plated, double hull of Brunel's supership surpassed the dimensions of Noah's fabled Ark and she was capable of carrying a staggering four thousand passengers.

The ship which the maritime world called the 'Wonder of the Seas', sported an unheard-of six masts and traditional maritime nomenclature could not be applied to them, so they were referred to as Monday, Tuesday, Wednesday, Thursday, Friday and Saturday. Motive power was to be supplied by a twenty-four-foot, steam-driven propeller, or gigantic paddle wheels, and, should her steam engines fail, the ship would simply unfurl her gargantuan sails. The Herculean vessel could also stockpile enough coal to power a journey from England to Australia and back without the need to refuel.

While the *Great Eastern* was under construction at Milwall, two hundred rivet gangs worked on the ship's novel double hull, until a staggering three million rivets had been firmly hammered into place. The outer hull was separated from the inner by a gap of three feet. Within the double hulls there was an innovative arrangement of sixteen watertight bulkheads, designed to make the ship virtually unsinkable.

One day in January 1857, during the round-the-clock racket of hammering and banging, somebody noticed that one of the riveters and his apprentice were missing. The weeks passed by, but the two missing men were nowhere to be found. Another riveter, an Irishman, reported that he had heard a strange pounding noise coming from within the double hull, but no one took him seriously and the noises were never investigated.

The width of the River Thames at the Millwall shipyards was not sufficient to allow the *Great Eastern* to be launched lengthways, so the ship had to be ushered into the river sideways; an operation that took an agonising three months, during which all kinds of technical difficulties were experienced. During this protracted procedure, Brunel became ill through overwork and worry. He was only fifty-three years old but looked at least twenty years older, through working for years without adequate sleep. He opened the *Times* newspaper one day to read, with bitterness, that the editor had dismissed his time-consuming project as a white elephant:

> *There she lies on the very brink of the noble river which is to carry her to the ocean, but she will not wet her lips.*

However, the leviathan finally did 'wet her lips' on 31 January 1858, after being eased three hundred and thirty feet down a slipway by buckling hydraulic jacks. Brunel himself remarked that, "Putting St Paul's to sea would have been easier!"

On the very day on which the *Great Eastern* was to be launched, Brunel was standing on deck, unable to believe that his magnificent creation was finally about to be put into service, when he suffered a massive stroke and collapsed. He remained gravely ill for the next year and a half and on 15 September 1859, he died, after hearing that a steam pipe had burst on the *Great Eastern* during her trial run to Weymouth. The massive explosion had destroyed a funnel and the searing cloud of escaping steam had boiled five stokers to death.

In a separate tragedy, at around the same time, another crewman had fallen on to a paddle wheel and been instantly smashed to pieces. Three members of the ship's crew had talked of hearing pounding noises within the hull just before the two tragedies took place.

The spiralling costs of the delayed launch were astronomical – over one million pounds – and quickly brought financial ruin to the Eastern Navigation Company, who had planned to employ Brunel's ship on long voyages to India and Australia. The Great Ship Company took over the project and opted instead for the quick profits of the North Atlantic run. From that point onwards, the unlucky career of the *Great Eastern* started in earnest. The first planned voyage to the United States in 1861 had to be cancelled because the repair work to the ship's damaged funnel and boiler took longer than expected.

The frustrated directors of the Great Ship Company were eager to get some return on their troublesome investment, so, as an interim measure, they moved the *Great Eastern* to Holyhead in Wales, to put her on display to paying sightseers. But, shortly after arriving at Holyhead, one of the fiercest gales in living memory tore in from the Irish Sea and ripped the mighty vessel from her moorings.

For eighteen agonising hours she was tossed about in the coastal waters, but she rode the storm well, while other ships sank all around her, thanks to her new-fangled double hull and waterproofed bulkheads. After the gale had moved away, the *Great Eastern* was an awesome sight, as she steamed majestically from the storm-clouded horizon, back to

Holyhead. However, she did not escape unscathed, as the storm had caused thousands of pounds worth of damage to the ship's grand saloon.

Three months later, the *Great Eastern's* first captain, William Harrison, the coxswain, along with the nine-year-old son of the chief purser, were all drowned, when a sudden violent storm swamped their gig as they were going ashore. In the seafaring world, nothing casts a darker shadow over a ship's character than the death of a captain prior to a maiden voyage. So, when the news of the three deaths reached London, the directors of the Great Ship Company resigned immediately.

After Captain Harrison's death the disasters associated with the ill-fated ship continued. She was hit by a hurricane in mid-Atlantic and she hit a rock near New York harbour which gashed a massive hole in her hull. The full story can be found in *Haunted Liverpool 4.*

Having been left to rust in Milford Haven harbour she was eventually towed to Birkenhead to be broken up and it was there that a most gruesome discovery was made. It was no easy task to break up the reinforced double hull of the ship, so the wreckers' iron ball was invented for the task. Three days into the formidable demolition job, the wreckers' ball dislodged a large plate. When the ball impacted into the ship again, something was seen to fall from a hole in the hull. Two demolition experts gave orders to cease work and went to investigate the object which had dropped out of the ship on to the piles of scrap at the quayside.

They were shocked to find that it was the skeleton of a man, draped in musky clothes. Another skeleton – that of a much younger male – was later found in another compartment, sandwiched between the two hulls. The skeletons were later formally identified as those of the missing riveter and his apprentice by members of their families who had travelled from Canning Town and Dagenham. Many believed that the chilling discovery explained the *Great Eastern's* jinxed history.

Now move southwards along the eastern side of the cemetery, and you will come upon the mysterious inscription 'LITTLE GRACE' engraved into a wall.

LITTLE GRACE

In Victorian times, there was a rumour that the four-year-old illegitimate daughter of a well-to-do gentleman was secretly buried in the dead of night in the cemetery after she had died from a short illness. To avoid a scandal, the clandestine nocturnal interment went ahead by the light of the moon, and the gravedigger was paid generously for his work. No marker was put on the grave, but shortly after the cloak and dagger burial, a girl of about four years of age, with a head of golden curls, and wearing a little white burial shroud, was often to be seen in broad daylight, standing by her secret grave. One couple allegedly saw a tiny child's hand reaching out from a small gap between two blocks in the wall. As they looked on in horror, the small hand withdrew back into the wall.

On another occasion, a man named Joseph Donough, a spiritual medium of some repute, was visiting the grave of a relative in St James's Cemetery, when the ghostly little girl appeared before him, accompanied by a fragrant scent of sweet violets. Donough enquired as to the girl's name, and the child said she had been known as little Grace, and told him where she was buried.

Donough somehow managed to trace Grace's father, presumably with the help of his psychic powers, and told him that he should be ashamed of burying his beautiful little daughter in an unmarked grave. The father of the deceased girl threatened to sue the medium, but Joseph Donough later went back to the cemetery and chiselled out the words 'LITTLE GRACE' in the wall for everyone who visited the graveyard to see. The medium then saw the child appear one day and announce that she was, "Going home to Jesus" and with that she smiled, waved, then instantly vanished.

From the Little Grace inscription, move a short distance south along the east wall of the cemetery until you come to Liverpool's only surviving running spring, first discovered by quarry workers in 1773.

THE SPRING

The water of the 'Liverpool Spa' was once sought by people afflicted with weak or inflamed eyes, and was also thought to cure rickets, 'crudities of the stomach' and 'lowness of spirits'.

The water contains trace elements of silica, calcium carbonate, calcium sulphate, magnesium nitrate, magnesium chloride and sodium carbonate. The spring is thought to course beneath Liverpool from the direction of Church Street. In January 1868, two thousand bodies were removed from St Peter's churchyard, in Church Street, as part of the work to widen the thoroughfare. When the coffins were being loaded on to a cart destined for Anfield Cemetery, several of them were in such a rotten state, that the cadavers within them became exposed, and two bodies which were extraordinarily intact, came to light.

One was that of a young woman who had died decades before, and she looked as if she was merely asleep, with no signs of decomposition whatsoever. Another body, that of Captain David Gwin, who had died on the 21 July 1813 aged seventy-six, resembled a grey statue, because his flesh was so stoney-looking. It was surmised that Gwin's corpse had become completely petrified because a mineral-laden spring had filtered through his coffin. It was noted that the spring was headed south, and was most likely the same one that still issues from the wall of St James's Cemetery. Above the spring you will see a stone plaque which reads thus:

Christian reader view in me,
An emblem of true charity,
Who freely what I have bestow,
Though neither heard nor seen to flow,
And I have full returns from Heaven,
For every cup of water given

Opposite the spring, you will see the towering, domed mausoleum of the William Huskisson MP, who died tragically on 15 September 1830, after being run over by George Stephenson's Rocket locomotive, thus becoming the first person in the world to be killed by a train.

HUSKISSON'S MAUSOLEUM

On that fateful day, the opening of the Liverpool to Manchester Railway was being marked by a procession of eight locomotives, all of them built by Stephenson. Around six-hundred guests took part in the event, with thousands of spectators present to cheer them along. William Huskisson was a guest of the Duke of Wellington, whose personal carriage was drawn up on one railway line at Parkside, near

Newton-Le-Willows, to review the procession passing by on the other track. However, eyewitnesses claimed that Huskisson and the Duke became involved in a heated political discussion and the Liverpool MP stormed from the carriage.

Seconds later, Huskisson was struck by the Rocket locomotive, which was steaming along at twenty-four mph and was horrifically injured. One of his legs was badly mangled and shattered by the wheels of the prototype train. As he lay by the track in a pool of blood, Huskisson went into shock and pronounced, "I have met my death". He was taken to the parsonage at Eccles aboard the locomotive *Northumbrian*, driven by George Stephenson himself at thirty-six mph, but the MP died in agony that night at 9pm.

Not long after Huskisson was laid to rest, there were sinister sightings of a man in black, wearing a top hat and a long cape, limping around St James's Cemetery, close to the Huskisson mausoleum, and some of those who had known the MP in life were convinced that it was his shade, restless perhaps because he was discontented with the political situation at that time. When the Duke of Wellington had become Prime Minister in 1828, Huskisson refused to serve under him and resigned from office.

Then, one warm August evening in 1973, a vagrant named Bob woke up in the grounds of St James's Cemetery after consuming two bottles of cheap but very potent wine. He dragged himself to his feet and staggered up a path that led to the main gate in the northern end of the cemetery. Bob discovered to his horror that this gate was padlocked. The tramp shouted to several passers-by, and some of them stopped, but nervously walked on again after surveying the scruffily dressed man peering through the railings in the dark. Bob stumbled through the eerie twilit landscape of the dead until he reached the other gate – only to find that it was locked too. Bob shook that gate and shouted, but no one came. The vagrant then recalled a missing railing at the eastern terrace of the cemetery and hurried off, desperate to find a means of escaping his terrifying predicament.

Bob passed the huge domed monument in the centre of the cemetery and momentarily paused there to regain his breath, when he heard a strange noise echoing all around him. Bob listened carefully, and realised that it was the sound of … of footsteps. Footsteps that were heading his way. Then he saw the source of those footsteps. It was the shadowy figure of a tall man who wore a long flowing cape and a top hat. The oddly dressed man was limping towards him, dragging its leg, less than thirty feet away. It muttered something unintelligible and reached out with its right hand. The white collar and cuffs of the backdated stranger were phosphorescent, yet the face seemed undefined and grey.

Bob ran off, suddenly feeling decidedly sober and felt his legs going weak as a wave of fear coursed through his nervous system. The top-hatted man, who was obviously a ghost, limped after the terror-stricken vagrant up a grassy incline towards the railing. Bob eventually found the gap after searching for what seemed like an eternity in a blind panic, but by then the limping ghost was closing in on him. As the caped apparition reached out to Bob, the vagrant screamed and just managed to squeeze his ragged form through the gap in the railings, scraping his back and chest in the process. He tumbled on to the pavement of Hope Street, then clambered to his feet and ran off to rejoin the company of the living.

The domed building where Bob encountered the ghost is the mausoleum of the Victorian MP William Huskisson, so perhaps his ghost was the limping spectre that Bob encountered on that August night in 1973.

From the Huskisson Mausoleum walk back towards the same side of the cemetery where the spring is (the eastern side), but this time go further south, towards the Upper Parliament Street end, where you will come across several walled-up arched entrances to tombs.

GRAVE DESECRATION

In the 1960s a few of these tombs were broken into and the desecraters stole jewellery and opened lead-lined coffins. The heinous crime came to light one evening when a policeman on his beat saw three young boys on Duke Street kicking a human skull about. The lads said they had found the skull in the nearby graveyard – St James's Cemetery.

The policeman, suspecting that a grave had been exhumed, went to investigate, and came upon a deplorable scene. One of the tombs built into the eastern wall had been smashed open with considerable force, as if a sledgehammer had been used. Inside, a red-haired girl of about six years of age was sitting up in a small lead coffin. The coffin lid had been wrenched off and curled back as if the casket was a sardine can. The policeman shone his torch at the girl and asked her who she was, thinking she was a living child for a few moments. Then he noticed that she was dressed in old-fashioned clothes. Part of her Titian plaited hair had been cut off, and pieces of an onyx necklace were strewn on the floor, where the desecraters had wrenched at the child's jewellery.

The constable noted that the child's eyes were closed, and she looked as if she was sleeping, and that, coupled with the fact that she was dressed in Victorian or Edwardian clothes, made him realise that she was in fact a corpse.

The policeman rushed out of the plundered tomb to summon assistance, and by the time a detective had arrived, the girl's body was starting to crumble and decay as the twentieth century air got to her. The detective took charge of the situation and was gently pushing the girl backwards, trying to ease her back into her damaged coffin, when her eyes plopped out of their sockets, one landing in the horrified detective's palm.

Handkerchiefs were held to mouths as the stench of decomposition worsened, turning the air thick and fetid. The tomb was sealed up once more, but within months, a neighbouring tomb was broken into. Again, jewellery was stolen, and the two corpses were disturbed, only this time, indecipherable symbols were found scrawled inside the tomb, on the walls and on the floor, and some believed these glyphs and drawings to be of an occult nature.

WALTER SLIM AND THE GRAVEROBBERS
FROM HAUNTED LIVERPOOL 8

The tomb of one Walter Slim (1861-1888) was also broken into years later, in August 1971, and the lid was removed from his coffin, but nothing was taken. On the floor of the tomb, police saw that someone had drawn a strange, star-like symbol with eight points. The story came to me when a former student of the University of Liverpool rang me one afternoon at the studios of Radio Merseyside to relate a tale I had heard something of before. I often hear several versions of an alleged supernatural event, and more often than not, I have to try and 'iron out' the inconsistencies of the varying accounts to avoid contradictions arising. The following story, however, was related to me over a period of almost three years, from no fewer than seven people, and all of their recollections regarding a very strange tale concurred entirely. The last piece of the jigsaw, which made the story complete, was the discovery of a name in a Liverpool cemetery which I happened to stumble upon. Without further ado, here is the eerie tale of Walter Slim.

On the evening of Friday 13 August 1971, at around nine o'clock, five male students left their lodgings on Liverpool's Upper Stanhope Street and headed for the Philharmonic pub on Hope Street. This was the so-called 'glam rock' era, with bands like T Rex appearing in the pop charts, and it wasn't unusual for the youth of the early seventies, especially students, to dress outlandishly. Two of the five students wore battered old top hats and Army trench-coats, and one even wore a deerstalker which sported a scarlet carnation. Fashion-wise, it was an era of anything goes.

The strangely-clad students decided to take a short cut through St James's cemetery, which, I'm sure you'll agree, is a creepy place even in broad daylight, but this was nine o'clock at night, and twilight heightened the supernatural menace of the vast graveyard. The students were glad when they had emerged unscathed on the other side of the cemetery, and they hurried past the Liverpool Institute (which is now the 'Fame' School, LIPA).

At this point, one of the students, Douggie, noticed a stranger walking alongside them, wearing a top hat and a long black opera cloak. He also sported a white starched collar and a large bow tie. He was about six feet in height, and looked about thirty years old. His face was extremely pallid and anaemic-looking. Douggie nudged one of his friends, grimaced and asked, "Who's he?"

His friend looked at the stranger and shrugged. The students crossed Hardman Street, but the stranger stood rooted to the kerb, gazing in fascination at the cars waiting at the traffic lights. Douggie and his friends entered the spacious lounge of the Philharmonic pub, which was packed on this Friday night. Then, as Douggie was ordering a drink, he saw the top-hatted man in the cloak dash into the pub, throw back his cloak and screech with laughter. He seemed demented, or possibly high on drugs. Everyone in the pub noticed the stranger and they all agreed that he was decidedly creepy. The barman looked him up and down and asked him what he wanted to drink, and in a strange-sounding voice the man replied, "In the name of human charity, I'll have your gin, sir!"

The barman enquired how he wanted the gin, and the man in the topper impatiently waved his hand and shouted, "Gin, sir! Nothing else!" and he slapped the counter three times with the palm of his hand. Everyone backed off, because there was something extremely sinister about the man. A lot of people later recalled how he had given off an overpowering body odour, mingled with a sickly sweet scent, reminiscent of violets. The glass of gin was duly poured and placed before the eccentric stranger, and the barman held out his hand, expecting to be paid, but the stranger ignored him, swigging down the neat, undiluted gin and banging the glass down on the counter.

He then turned around and walked to a corner where a black girl was standing on her own. The girl was exceptionally beautiful and wore her hair in the popular 'Afro' style. She backed up against the wall as the malodorous man approached. He grabbed her hand, kissed her knuckle, and simultaneously tilted his hat. "My name is Walter Slim," he said, and his dark eyes seemed to smile, though his lips did not move. He asked the girl her name.

"Sarah," she said, very self-consciously.

"What a delightful name!" Walter chimed, and began to ramble on about how his father had supported the campaign to end the despicable institution of slavery. He then lapsed into sentimentality, and in a choked-up voice, he said, "Many, many years ago, I loved a girl named Sarah. The beautiful Miss Sarah Beaton."

Walter then produced a beautiful silver locket and opened it to show Sarah the oval portrait within of a young golden-haired lady. Tears rolled down Walter's face as he described how Sarah had died from a fever, just days before he was due to marry her. She had been just seventeen. The twentieth century Sarah felt great sympathy for the smelly stranger, and subconsciously realised that he must be some sort of flesh and blood ghost. For some reason she was no longer afraid.

"I feel quite ill," Walter said suddenly.

At this point, the barman, who had been diddled out of his money, told him to get out, saying that he was permanently barred. Walter stumbled out of the pub into the night, with Sarah following him. Her friends begged her not to go after him, because he was obviously mad, but she ignored them and set off after him. She followed him to the cemetery nestling in the shadow of the looming Gothic splendour of the massive sandstone Anglican Cathedral, and she immediately noticed how he seemed terrified of the traffic plying its way along Rodney Street. Sarah squinted into the darkness and watched him stagger into the blackness until he could no longer be seen. She was afraid of the dark at the best of times and wisely decided against following him into the cemetery alone.

Well, that should have been that. The incident went down in Liverpool folklore; the far-fetched tale of Walter Slim. The Victorian ghost who called in for a gin at the Philharmonic pub, had even reached my young ears when I was a child living off nearby Myrtle Street. Some thought the visitation was a hoax, staged by some madcap student with a dark sense of humour on that Friday the thirteenth.

Then, one evening in July 2002, I was in the Everyman Bistro when I happened to meet a man named Ken, who had once been a photographer for the *Liverpool Echo* many years before. We chatted on the subject of the paranormal, and Ken mentioned that he had once been called out to take a photograph of a huge, eight-pointed, occult symbol, which black magicians had drawn in the cellar of the derelict John Bagot Hospital in the north of the city. The dabblers in the Black Arts had drawn up the symbol in the old hospital, because so many people had died there over the years, and the occultists probably wanted to try and channel the energy that had been released at that location to open up a portal to demonic entities.

Ken later produced the actual photograph. I had seen the strange symbols in the photograph somewhere before. I checked them against a photograph I had in my possession of an identical eight-pointed star scrawled in the desecrated tomb of a Victorian gentleman in the Cathedral cemetery off Hope Street in 1971. When I checked the name on this tomb, I saw that it read: 'Walter Slim, 1861-1888'. He had died at the tender age of twenty-seven. I then remembered the old tale about the ghost walking into the Philharmonic pub. The other name mentioned had been a Sarah Beaton. I also located her grave in the same cemetery. She had died in 1885, aged seventeen.

The occultists who had broken into Walter Slim's tomb had carried out one of the most controversial and terrifying rituals in black magic, the 'Octagenesis of Resurrection', which is purported to be a way of raising the dead. However, the revived corpse usually disintegrates after an hour or so. Only perfectly preserved corpses, taken from a lead-lined coffin, are used in the ritual. Walter Slim was laid to rest in just such a lead coffin …

Now leave the tombs and walk back towards the Huskisson Mausoleum, and continue past it until you come to a row of gravestones that are situated at the bottom of a steep wooded slope. If you look carefully, you will see the headstones above the mass grave of young children who were looked after at the Myrtle Street Orphanage.

GHOSTLY URCHINS

In January 2005, several people walking through the cemetery saw a group of children all dressed in black, a few of them wearing flat caps, near to these graves. One woman, named Jo, was walking her dog through the cemetery at around 9am, when she suddenly saw four male children, aged around seven to ten years of age, standing in a line, gazing at her. Two of these children were barefoot and all of them held each other's hands as they looked on. The woman's dog wagged its tail and lunged at the ghosts, but Jo, sensing that there was something supernatural about the four youngsters, stopped in her tracks and held the animal back by its leash. A moment later, the spectral boys had vanished.

What were probably the same four ghostly children were later seen by several people in the same area, but this time all of the sightings were in the evening. A medium wrote to me several years ago to say that she had often been accompanied on her walks through the cemetery by four ghostly urchins, and one of these manifested spirits told her that his name was John Twist. The boy was surprisingly cheerful, but he and the three others seemed to be hiding from someone or something, and kept looking about as they were in the medium's company. If you look at the orphans' gravestones you will indeed come across one with an inscription which states that a John Twist died on 3 December 1861, aged just twelve years of age.

From the orphan graves, walk northwards, back towards the place where you entered the cemetery, but stop about twenty feet before you reach the corner leading to the arched entrance. Now look up the wooded slope towards the cathedral.

PILLAR OF SHADOW

A very strange apparition has been seen ascending and descending this slope over the years. It takes the form of a black, vaporous, elongated object, also described as a 'pillar of shadow' by some witnesses.

I saw this unusual apparition myself when I was conducting a ghost tour on behalf of the *Daily Post* in October 2003. Dusk was gathering, and I was standing at Huskisson's Mausoleum, at the end of the ghost walk, facing the slope as I told the story of the limping spectre, when I suddenly became aware of something black slowly descending the slopes to my right. I became distracted by the eerie object, and several people present noticed that I was becoming fixated with something and turned around to see what I was gazing at. There were nervous gasps of surprise as they too saw the cylindrical dark shape come to a halt. I felt as if this entity was watching us, perhaps wondering what we were all doing in the cemetery during the hours of dusk. Seconds later, the pillar of darkness drifted slowly back up the slope and vanished among the shadowy trees and gnarled bare branches.

I rushed over to the spot where we had seen the unearthly apparition, and tried to rationalise it, but to no avail. I noted the short stump of a tree, and wondered whether, in the darkness, it could have been perceived as something more sinister through some trick of the light. But by no stretch of the imagination could a short, two-foot tall tree stump be transformed into a moving elongated shadow at least eight feet in height. Perhaps a black polythene garbage bag had been blown up and down the slopes in the sharp October wind? I saw no such bag and quickly eliminated that unlikely possibility too. As I stood pondering the nature of the apparition, most people had hurried away from the cemetery, unnerved by the sinister 'thing' we had glimpsed in the woods of the slope. If you find yourself in the cemetery, by the slope, when the shadows are lengthening, look out for the 'pillar of shadow'!

RODNEY STREET (LEFT-HAND SIDE)

If you are still feeling brave enough to continue the walk, leave St James's Cemetery, and walk back down Rodney Street, crossing over at Hardman Street. Stay on the right-hand side of Rodney Street, and you will come to a row of houses that runs from Number 13 to Number 17. These houses were used as a nursing home in the past, and throughout the years, various ghosts have been sighted in the buildings, including phantom nuns.

One ghost, in particular, has been repeatedly seen by many different people – the terrifying apparition of a girl in a white nightgown, or possibly a burial shroud. Many encounters with the girl describe her with staring dark-rimmed eyes and slit wrists, from which blood flows copiously. The blood, like the girl, vanishes after dripping on the stairs of the house at Number 17. Lights switch on and off at the houses that were once part of the nursing home, and phantom crying is also occasionally heard, along with phantom footsteps on the stairs. In Victorian times, nuns ran a home for unmarried mothers, and the ghost of the girl with the slit wrists is thought to be that of Polly Burrows.

POLLY

Around the mid-1970s, a spate of ghostly activity broke out at the nursing home at which stretched from Number 13 to Number 17 Rodney Street, and one of the first people to witness the supernatural goings-on was the matron, but she chose to say nothing at first, for fear of alarming the staff and patients.

However, a young nurse called Brenda was working on the nightshift one January evening at eleven o'clock, when she heard the sounds of what seemed to be a woman sobbing somewhere in the upper floors of the house. At first, Brenda thought it was a patient, but then she heard the dull footfall of someone coming down the stairs. Waiting in suspense at the foot of the stairs, Brenda saw the crying woman reach the landing above and turn to face her as she came down the staircase.

The woman was dressed from head to toe in white, and was aged between twenty and twenty-five years of age. The long, white, featureless garment was like an old-fashioned night-gown. Brenda's heart pounded, because the woman was partly transparent, and not only was her face as pale as chalk, there were two dark lines across her wrists, and blood was flowing copiously from the gashes. The phantom's ethereal cheeks glistened as tears flowed from a pair of large, black, sorrowful eyes. Brenda suddenly realised that the 'night-gown' she was wearing was almost certainly a burial shroud.

Filled with a rising sensation of terror, the nurse turned, and found herself running down the stairs, unable to cry out. The ghost followed her down, and Brenda fled into the dark empty office that was occupied by the matron during the day. The nurse was so petrified that she slammed the door and cowered under the desk, and listened in dread as the sounds of sobbing got nearer and nearer. The ghost passed straight through the closed door, and walked towards the desk. The apparition was so vivid that Brenda could clearly see its bare, ashen feet standing by the desk. She screwed her eyes tightly shut and fervently made the sign of the cross – and when she opened them, the ghost had vanished. When she was sure that the ghost had finally left the office, she switched on every light in the building and alerted two other nurses. That night, the three nurses on duty were so frightened that there might be a repetition of the ghostly apparition, that they even refused to go to the toilet alone.

The next day, Brenda told the matron about the woman in white with the slashed wrists, expecting her superior to be sceptical. To her surprise, the matron revealed that she had also seen the woman in white at the nursing home – exactly three years before, on the 9 January. The matron revealed that she had always been a bit psychic, but had never told anyone about her gift, for fear of being ridiculed. When she had seen the spectre coming down the stairs, for some reason she had received the strong impression that the troubled ghost's name was Polly. Matron had also experienced an overpowering feeling of a sadness and misery which had made her throat close up. Then, seconds afterwards, the wraith-like woman had melted away.

Rather than putting her mind at rest, this new information made Brenda feel even more uneasy, because it confirmed that the nursing home was haunted, and therefore she could be confronted by the ghostly woman at any time. News of the haunting spread through the home and beyond, and one of the cleaners who had worked there in the past said that she had once seen the vivid ghost of a nun walking up the same stairs with her back to her.

From that day onwards, Brenda refused point blank to do night shifts, and even during the day her nerves remained taut while she was on duty.

At around this time, Brenda started dating John David, whose unusual hobby was ghost hunting. He possessed all the recommended equipment for this strange pastime, and he often worked with a medium named Bill Holroyd, an epileptic young man who had quite a reputation for 'empathising' with ghosts. Unlike most mediums, Holroyd refused to be paid for a gift which he claimed had been bestowed on him by 'a higher authority'.

Naturally, Brenda's boyfriend was fascinated by her encounter with the woman in white, and constantly asked her if he could investigate the case for her. She said that he'd have to check with the matron. She refused his request at first, but later relented, when the ghost continued to make alarming appearances at the home, frightening all her staff. The matron said John and his mediumistic associate would be allowed access for a few hours, on condition that they kept a low profile, and promised not to talk to anyone from the newspapers. John and Bill gave their word that they wouldn't seek any media attention.

About a week later, just before midnight, Bill warned the three nurses on night duty to stay in their staffroom. The ghost was about to walk, he told them, and he was right. First came the sorrowful crying sound – then the pale, pathetic figure started to descend the stairs. John waited with a camera loaded with infra red film halfway up the stairs and he clicked on his audio cassette recorder. Bill Holroyd bravely intercepted the ghost on the stairs, wondering if it would walk right through him, but instead the ghost halted and gazed at him with a look of indescribable anguish. Bill whispered to her – questions about her name, and why she was so restless. Almost four minutes elapsed, and during that eternity of heightened suspense, John saw the girl's mouth faintly flicker. Then she slowly faded away, and Bill reached out slowly to touch the air where she had stood.

The medium came downstairs and imparted all of the information he had received from the ghost. Her name was Mary Burrows, but she had been known as Polly to her family and friends. She had lived locally in Falkner Square with her sisters and father and she had been deeply in love with a poor carpenter named Samuel. Polly had become pregnant with his child, and her father had been so outraged, that he had had Samuel dragged into a solicitor's office, where he was pressed into signing a contract which promised that he would receive a large sum of money if he would stop seeing Polly.

Samuel had chosen the money instead of Polly.

Having a child out of wedlock was regarded as scandalous in Victorian times, permanently ruining a girl's reputation. Polly was locked away in a convent and put in the care of the nuns. After the birth, the nuns gave the baby away to a childless couple. Polly was convinced that Samuel would come and rescue her, but after months of waiting, she realised that he no longer cared for her, and in utter despair she slashed her wrists.

All of this information was checked and verified. The electoral registers were examined, and it was established that in Victorian times nuns did indeed run a home for unmarried mothers at the Rodney Street house which was presently occupied by the nursing home.

Further research also ascertained that a Burrows family had lived in Falkner Square during that period. The medium spent almost a week at the nursing home, trying his utmost to persuade the tormented spirit of Polly Burrows to pass over to the world of peaceful spirits where she belonged, but she refused, and as far as I know, Polly still haunts the house on Rodney Street where she took her life in a moment of intense heartache.

Cross over to 16 Rodney Street, where the Puschka restaurant now stands.

ROMAINE OF RODNEY STREET
FROM HAUNTED LIVERPOOL 6

In the 1920s and 1930s, a very strange individual named Alaric Romaine lived in this house at Number 16 Rodney Street. At the same time, in the front page columns of the *Liverpool Echo*, Romaine was advertised as 'a private detective who gets results'. Romaine is something of a mystery – he was described as being of foreign appearance – some said he was Hungarian. What was unusual about him was his unorthodox methods of detection. He claimed that he could occasionally read minds. He also maintained that he had an ability to receive psychic impressions from objects found at the scene of the crime, enabling him to piece together what had happened.

In January 1930, a woman called Clara Simmons called on Mr Romaine at his Rodney Street office. She showed him a photograph of a handsome-looking man with a pencil moustache and told him that it was her brother Robert. Clara recounted how she had had a petty argument with him a year ago and that he had not been in touch with her since. She asked Romaine if he could use his unique powers to locate him.

Romaine then did a curious thing. He asked Clara if he could study her palm. She consented and offered him her hand. With his finger, Romaine gently traced the fine lines on the woman's palm. However, this was actually Romaine's gimmick for reading a person's mind. He had learned this technique from the Indian fortune tellers during his days in Delhi. The Indian fakirs distract a person by getting them to focus their attention on their hand, and when a person drops his guard in this way it is supposedly possible to read their mind.

Romaine suddenly dropped the woman's hand.

"Robert isn't your brother, Miss Simmons, he's your lover!" he declared dramatically. " And you are a married woman." Clara Simmons gasped with shock, but Romaine persisted. "You are carrying his baby and he has deserted you. You want me to find him, of course."

Miss Simmons ended her charade and gave a little sob. Romaine felt pity for her and said, "The father of your child lives on the south coast now. I see water. At a guess, I'd say Bournemouth or Brighton."

Clara said that this was highly likely and she confided that Robert's family came from Boscombe – a suburb of Bournemouth. Whether Clara ever caught up with her errant lover is unknown.

On another occasion, a Mr Ling, from Chinatown, visited Romaine and said that someone had been stealing from his home. Mr Ling could not go to the police because he kept large amounts of opium on the premises, which had also been stolen. Romaine visited the scene of the crime and picked up a sort of psychic trail, like a bloodhound following its nose. The trail led to Mr Ling's brother-in-law. Mr Ling was furious and called Romaine a charlatan, but Romaine stayed perfectly calm and told Mr Ling to check the cellar of his brother-in-law's house. And, sure enough, in the cellar's floor safe, Mr Ling retrieved the stolen opium and other expensive items taken from his home.

In 1939, upon the outbreak of war, Romaine was summoned to

Whitehall, to help the fight against the Nazis in an amazing operation code-named 'Green Mirror'. Romaine and a group of skilled magicians and illusionists, including a gifted music hall conjuror, Jasper Maskelyne, hid tanks, armies and even an entire harbour full of ships. If you write to the Public Records Office and ask to see copies of the files on Romaine or Maskelyne, the London bureaucrats will tell you that the files are not due to be released until 2021. However, here are a few of the things that Romaine and the magicians did for the war effort: he somehow created images of British warships in the English Channel and made Montgomery's hundred and fifty thousand troops, with one thousand guns and tanks, invisible to Rommel, but Romaine and Maskelyne's greatest achievement was making an entire harbour vanish. This was Alexandria Harbour in Egypt. They simply had all the harbour lights turned off, and the magicians then recreated the same pattern of lights in the desert. Around these lights Romaine ordered explosive charges to be laid. When the German bombers flew over Alexandria, they found the harbour to be further to the west than they had expected and recalibrated their instruments. Then, as they started dropping bombs, Romaine set off the explosives around the lights, so that it looked as if both cargo and ships were going up in flames. The real harbour, a few miles to the east, survived the night raid.

These are just some examples of what Romaine of Rodney Street was involved in, but, in 2021, the world will finally discover the full truth about him.

Now cross back over to the other side of Rodney Street, and linger at the railings enclosing the churchyard of St Andrew's Scottish kirk, dominated by the huge pyramidal tomb of William James Mckenzie, whose ghost still walks during the hours of dusk.

THE RODNEY STREET SPECTRE
FROM HAUNTED LIVERPOOL 4

Early one morning in 1970, a middle-aged woman who worked as a kitchen assistant at the YMCA in Mount Pleasant, boarded the 86 bus near her home in Parliament Street at 6.30 in the morning. At Leece Street, the woman left the bus and headed for her place of work via Rodney Street. She had been taking this route every work day for over six years and was well accustomed to the spooky aura that hung over the site of the derelict ruins of St Andrew's Presbyterian Church. By now, she considered herself to be quite immune to the eerie atmosphere emanating from that part of Rodney Street.

As she neared the old church ruins, she suddenly found herself confronted with the solid-looking apparition of a top-hatted man in a cape, who came out of one of the walls that surrounded the church's cemetery. The ghost advanced towards the terrified woman, then hesitated, performed a U-turn and hurried back through the wall. Understandably, the woman took to her heels and quickly put as much distance as she could between herself and the spooky gentleman.

The identity of the ghost, which has been seen by many people over the years, including a policeman, the early morning milkman, postmen, homeward-bound clubbers, nightwatchmen and prostitutes, will probably never be known. However, not far from the spot where it emerged from the wall, in the grounds of the cemetery itself, stands the giant, sinister-looking, pyramidal tomb of a Scot called McKenzie, who was a wealthy promoter of the early railways and a restless advocate of scientific progress. Perhaps it is he who is restless still ...

In December 1999, I received a letter from a very old woman who divulged an incredible tale that she had heard regarding the spectre in Rodney Street, which she said had been passed down for generations. This letter, together with the years I have spent researching the Rodney Street apparition, have revealed that the ghost has a long and chequered history and my account is derived from all these sources.

One cold, foggy, Sunday night in the autumn of 1871, sixty-eight-year-old Lionel Harland, a respected Rodney Street doctor, left his surgery and was walking up Maryland Street, when he heard footsteps approaching ahead of him. The shadowy figure of a tall, wiry man wearing a top hat and a flowing cape, was emerging from the swirling fog, a hundred yards in front of him. Dr Harland hesitated at the corner of Maryland and Rodney Street and felt a cold shiver run up his spine, even though he was wearing a heavy fur coat on that chilly September night. The silhouette advanced towards him with an almost military gait and, as it came within range of the flickering yellow flame of a lamppost, the elderly doctor realised, to his horror, that the figure was the very same one that he had encountered twenty years previously. In fact, it was not a living person at all, but the ghastly-looking shade of a dead man – a man the doctor had known personally many years ago.

It was the terrifying apparition of James McKenzie, a corrupt and wicked character, who had gambled with the Devil and lost his soul as a result. He was now forever condemned to walk the earth without rest until Judgment Day.

Before the doctor could step off the pavement and cross the cobbled road to get away from the terrifying ghost, the apparition let out a spiteful cackle and sneeringly spat out the words: "Ha! Hospital Sunday!" referring to a charity collection which the doctor held on Sundays, to raise funds for poor people needing hospital treatment.

When he was halfway across the road, Dr Harland was brave enough to steal a single glance back at the cursed phantom and he almost passed out with fear. He noted, with horror, that McKenzie's face looked as if it was lit up by a crimson flame and his eyes were ink-black and lifeless. As the doctor shivered, the funereal figure drifted straight through the wall of the cemetery.

The trembling doctor reached the house of his friend, Daniel Jackson, in Blackburne Place and, after giving a garbled account of his meeting with McKenzie's ghost, he clutched his heart in agony and collapsed like a stone on to the hearth rug. Mr Jackson and a servant managed to revive him for a time and gave him a large shot of brandy. Dr Harland nodded, then managed to gasp out a few last words to his friend.

"Tell Brocklebank ... tell him about McKenzie ... He knows the story."

Moments later, without uttering anything further, the surgeon died in the fireside armchair.

The only Brocklebank whom Daniel Jackson knew of, was the wealthy philanthropist and ship-owner, Ralph Brocklebank. Therefore, after his friend's funeral, he forwarded a letter to the local tycoon, recounting the strange story of Dr Harland, but he was not confident of receiving a reply. He certainly did not expect a personal visit from the affluent Mr Brocklebank in response to his correspondence.

The seventy-year-old millionaire paid his unexpected visit to Mr Jackson's house, shortly before 11pm. He alighted from a hansom cab in an anonymous black Ulster coat, with a black felt fedora pulled down over his eyes. Brocklebank was led into the drawing room by a servant, whom he rudely dismissed with a wave of the hand. Daniel Jackson offered his illustrious guest a finely-cut tumbler of Hoagland's eight-year-old Scotch Whisky, rumoured to be Brocklebank's favourite tipple, but the mogul shook his head and, in a cavalier manner, he asked his host to go over the story which he had related in the letter.

As Mr Jackson delivered his account of Dr Harland's final moments

Brocklebank became more and more agitated. He perched on the edge of the fireside armchair, rhythmically jabbing the glowing coals of the fire with a poker, his face etched with tension. After he had listened to Mr Jackson, he, in turn, recounted a very strange story indeed, which threw some light on the McKenzie ghost. It was a tale of greed, murder and the supernatural. Brocklebank seemed to be almost seeing the events which he described in the flames of the grate as he spoke:

"I remember James McKenzie well. He was one of those people who seem to be born old and crooked. Even when he was in his fifties he looked decrepit. I was twenty-five years old when I first met him and your deceased friend was twenty-three and fresh out of medical school. McKenzie made and lost fortunes that most men can only dream of. He backed the early railways and financed George Stephenson's locomotive machines. He was regarded as a pillar of the community and a financial backer of commerce and industry; but there was another, deeply unsavoury, side to the man, of which few people were aware. He was a compulsive gambler and an intractable atheist. Someone told me that he had flung his family Bible on to the fire, after his sweetheart had died from a fever. They say he hated God because of her death.

"And there were many other strange rumours surrounding the man. In 1826, eleven bodies were found in barrels in the cargo hold of a ship at Liverpool Docks. The police traced the barrels to a house at Number 8 Hope Street; that house was being looked after by a James MacGowan, who was an associate of James McKenzie. Anyway, the police arrested MacGowan after they discovered twenty-two corpses, of men, women and children, which had been dug up from the local cemetery.

"MacGowan refused to name names, but everyone suspected McKenzie of being the instigator. There were whispers that he had turned the premises into a body-snatcher's warehouse, where the corpses were pickled in barrels, ready to be shipped off to medical schools in Scotland. The going rate was fifteen pounds per corpse, be it a man, woman or baby.

"In October 1850, something happened which I will never forget. McKenzie became acquainted with a mysterious gentleman known only as Mr Madison. Madison was the sharpest poker player he had ever met and on this memorable occasion, they played a game throughout the night. McKenzie lost everything to the unbeatable Madison. Just before dawn, weary and defeated, he was making preparations to leave, when Madison came up with a bizarre proposal.

'One more game, Mr McKenzie, Sir?' he suggested.

McKenzie was literally penniless by this point and admitted that he had nothing left to gamble.

'What about your soul?' persisted Madison.

'This is nay time for jests, please leave.'

But Madison made it plain that he was not joking. McKenzie nervously declined and said to him, 'I think I know who you are.'

'If you, Sir, are an atheist, then what have you to lose? For a man who does not believe in a creator cannot believe he was given a soul.' McKenzie was too proud to acknowledge the existence of the Almighty and the fool played a game of poker for his soul, which Madison won. James McKenzie fell to his knees with fear when his opponent, who was really the Devil, presented his winning hand and laughed with scorn.

'Fear not, vain and defeated one. I will not take your soul until you are laid to rest in your grave.

"When McKenzie glanced up, his tormentor had vanished without trace, leaving behind the acrid aroma of something burning in the room. This explains why Mr McKenzie was entombed in his little pyramid above ground sitting up at a card table with a winning poker hand. It was his desperate attempt to cheat the Devil out of claiming his soul. As long as McKenzie's mortal remains are above ground, Lucifer cannot claim his soul. But, because he rejected eternal rest with God, he has condemned himself to walk the night as a restless ghost until Judgment Day.

As old Mr Brocklebank was leaving the house in Blackburne Place, Daniel Jackson turned to him to ask him one last question.

"Sir, did you actually meet – Mr Madison?"

Before the millionaire walked off into the jade green fog, he solemnly nodded his head.

"You don't think I accumulated my wealth through hard work do you? But I'll have the Devil to pay when my time comes."

MOUNT PLEASANT

Remain on this side of Rodney Street and walk until you come to the corner where Rodney Street meets Mount Pleasant. Here, another Celtic shade has recently been sighted.

THE GHOSTLY SCOTSMAN
OF MOUNT PLEASANT

On Sunday 10 July 2005, at around 7pm, two female students waiting for a lift on Mount Pleasant couldn't help but notice an outlandish-looking Scotsman wearing a kilt, standing outside Reid of Liverpool bookshop (at 105 Mount Pleasant), peering through the shutters. As well as the kilt, the six-foot-tall Scot's outfit included a sporran, a Tam o'Shanter with a feather, and what looked like a ceremonial sword. The girls thought the man looked old fashioned with his turned-up moustache and odd mannerisms. As they were about to climb into a friend's car, the Scotsman asked them if they knew the whereabouts of a Doctor Bligh. They said they didn't, and the Celtic stranger walked towards the corner of nearby Pomona Street – and literally vanished into thin air in front of their eyes.

A witness from a nearby hotel named Philip also saw the ghostly Scotsman standing outside the bookshop, as well as several other premises on Mount Pleasant. Philip, a retired soldier, told me:

"The figure which I and many other people have seen was wearing the old uniform of the King's Liverpool Regiment, and knowing my military history, I would say he belonged to the Tenth Scottish Battalion. The sword he carries would put him in a Victorian time-frame. One morning, around six o'clock I woke up in my hotel room to hear bagpipe music playing somewhere close by, and I later heard the same strange pipes on Pomona Street. It is quite eerie."

I researched the houses on Mount Pleasant with which the spectral Scot seems obsessed, and I was very intrigued to discover that a Dr John Bligh, MD, did indeed have a surgery at 109 Mount Pleasant in the 1880s. Just why the shade of a Scottish soldier from a bygone era should materialise and go in search of a long-dead doctor, is anybody's guess. Ghosts often 'come out of the woodwork' when a building is altered, or land is disturbed, and at the time of the haunting, the Big Dig workers had been excavating in the area where the phantom soldier was active. A taxi driver travelling up Mount Pleasant in his cab at 11pm on the Friday night of 12 August 2005, saw the same Caledonian phantasm standing at the Clarence Street junction, looking down towards Rodney Street where, of course, the other spectre of Scottish lineage – William McKenzie – patrols the night-time streets.

CLARENCE STREET

Now cross Mount Pleasant and enter Clarence Street, which was given its name in 1809 when the Duke of Clarence visited the town. Stay on the right-hand side of Clarence Street and go to Number 27, the scene of a mysterious murder attempt in the summer of 1881, which was solved by Gloria Hamlet, a female detective whom I first introduced to my readers in Haunted Liverpool 8.

SAVED BY A BEE
FROM HAUNTED LIVERPOOL 9

Mrs Gloria Hamlet, and her trusty side-kick, Florrie Perkins between them, tackled many intriguing crimes. After being widowed at the age of twenty-nine, Mrs Hamlet left her Cheshire home and moved to Liverpool, where she set up a small chandler's shop in Bold Street.

Florrie helped in the shop, as well as delivering purchases to customers' homes on her bicycle. Mrs Hamlet and Florrie Perkins obviously loved the challenge of solving local mysteries, amongst them the following bizarre tale.

One beautiful sunny evening in June 1881, at precisely 7pm, a thirty-one-year-old mathematics tutor, Lawrence Williams, was leaning out of the window of his top-floor Clarence Street lodgings as usual, enjoying the view and smoking his pipe. As he puffed away, idly watching the people and carriages passing by below – a huge bumble bee came buzzing through the air directly towards him. Williams batted the bee away with his pipe – and at precisely the same time, there was a loud bang in the street. A bullet whizzed past the maths teacher's head, grazing his cheek and shattering the mirror on his dresser. Williams dived for cover, and when his landlady Mrs Bronte came rushing into the room, he screamed at her to stay away from the window and dive for cover.

There were no more shots, and the police were soon on the scene. The bullet had been of a .44 calibre, and one detective suspected that the Fenians – an Irish terrorist group – could be behind the shooting. Only a week earlier the Irishmen had attempted to dynamite Liverpool Town Hall for their cause: Home rule for Ireland. The houses on the opposite side of Clarence Street were painstakingly searched, but no trace of any gunman could be found, although they did uncover one possible lead, but it wasn't pursued as thoroughly as it could have been.

The window in a lodging house facing Williams's room had been left open, and the lodger – a Mr Sylvester – hadn't been seen since he left at eight o'clock that morning. His room was checked, and although a faint aroma of cordite hung in the air, no gun was found. The landlord said that Sylvester had paid a month's rent in advance. He had been a very small, quiet, inoffensive-looking man, yet other lodgers confirmed that the gunshot had definitely originated in his room. Nothing seemed to add up, as Sylvester's room had been empty and locked at the time of the shooting, and no one was seen, or heard, to run from it. The landlord had rushed upstairs immediately after hearing the tremendous bang, and he had passed no one on his way up. If the gunshot had indeed come from that room, then the gunman must have been invisible.

Detectives then asked Williams if he knew of anyone who would want to harm him. The teacher thought long and hard, but couldn't think of anyone who might have a grudge against him. The strange incident was gradually forgotten, the police having decided that the whole thing had been an accidental shooting by someone messing about with a pistol, which did not warrant further investigation.

Mrs Gloria Hamlet, however, was not one to let a mystery rest and became fascinated by the incident. She not only interviewed Williams, but also visited the lodging house where the mysterious would-be assassin was thought to have had a room. The landlord took a liking to the attractive-looking detective, and upon her second visit to the lodging house he admitted – over a glass of sherry – that he had found two objects in the room which had been abandoned by the mysterious Mr Sylvester: a book of illustrated nursery rhymes, left open at a certain page, and a beautiful, expensive-looking clock – not the sort of item which could have easily been overlooked, even if the person was leaving in a hurry.

Mrs Hamlet inspected the clock, which was a French Japy Frères model, eighteen inches in height, and she admired its quality. Then she turned to the book of nursery rhymes. The purple ribbon in the book had been left in the page that displayed the following verse:

There was a little man and he had a little gun,
And his bullets were made of lead, lead, lead;
He went to the brook, and shot a little duck,
Right through the middle of its head, head, head.

Perhaps the rhyme contained some kind of deliberate clue, Mrs Hamlet mused. She examined the clock, and noticed that the silver medallion on its front slid sideways. She then gazed through a hole in the back of the timepiece – and was shocked to discover that she was looking through a cross-haired gun-sight. The clock was carefully dismantled, and found to contain a .44 percussion revolver, with its trigger tied to a lever amongst the timepiece's cogs. The clock had been set up to fire the gun at 7pm – long after Mr Sylvester had left his lodgings for good.

The intended victim – Mr Williams – shuddered when he was told of Mrs Hamlet's findings, and he suddenly remembered the comical-looking 'midget' whom he and a friend had made fun of some three weeks before the shooting. Filled with shame, he admitted that they had belly-laughed at the diminutive man as he passed below the window. The only excuse that he could come up with for his deplorable behaviour was that he and his friend had been drinking and were quite tipsy that evening.

Williams was a man of habit, and each evening, at precisely 7pm, he could be seen smoking his pipe at his window. The little man must have noticed this and, inwardly seething because of Williams's insensitive behaviour, had plotted his ingenious revenge. It could have been the perfect murder, had the bullet struck its target squarely. Instead, a humble bumble bee had saved the life of Lawrence Williams.

Mr Sylvester was never traced. He was undoubtedly a warped genius, and I have the unsettling feeling that he may have actually killed before – and after – the mysterious Clarence Street shooting. Perhaps his murders were executed so cleverly, that they were made to look like accidents.

The house from which the bullet was lethally fired from its clockwork gun was owned by Donald Watson, and no longer stands today. Liverpool Community College now occupies the spot where the house once stood.

Staying on the Right side of Clarence Street, walk just one door down, to Number 25, and here you will see the house which was occupied by a jeweller named Burrows, in the 1880s.

RED GNOME

Number 25 Clarence Street became the destination for a chilling delivery in 1858. It all began earlier that year, when the one hundred and thirty-eight-foot long, three hundred and eighty-five-ton wooden brig called the *Black Hawk*, built by Stevens and Presley of Ohio City, sailed from Detroit, Michigan, to Liverpool, laden with a very strange cargo. Down in the hold, stowed away among the nineteen thousand bushels of corn and padded parcels of stained glass, there was a barrel containing the pickled corpse of something truly terrifying.

Before I relate just what that thing was, let me take you back over two centuries in time and three thousand six hundred miles away in space, to the days of the early settlers in Detroit.

In June 1763, British Captain James Dalyell and fifty-eight of his officers, were followed near the banks of Detroit River by a small, misshapen, crimson-clad figure with penetrating eyes, a large, fanged mouth, and a hideous, scarlet-veined face. Several soldiers shot at the weird-looking figure, but he vanished into the dense undergrowth of the wilderness. An old trapper warned Captain Dalyell and his men that they were being stalked by what the French settlers called the 'Nain Rouge' – the Red Gnome – a sinister supernatural entity whose appearance foretold misfortune and death.

Sure enough, shortly after seeing the crimson dwarf, Captain Dalyell and his soldiers were ambushed and massacred by the Indian Chief, Pontiac, and the blood of those slain turned the tributary of the Detroit River red for days. Decades earlier, the founder of Detroit, Antoine de la Mothe Cadillac, was also unlucky enough to encounter the Red Gnome, and soon lost his vast fortune and political standing. The diminutive omen of impending misfortune and death was seen again in 1801, shortly before the wooden city of Detroit was destroyed by a fire. Then, in the War of 1812, the Nain Rouge was seen prowling about in a fog by many witnesses, including General William Hull, who was forced to hand over Detroit to the British troops days later.

Around the end of 1857, there was a rumour circulating that two hunters had killed the Red Gnome in a forest. They had shot him several times and then fixed him to a tree with their bayonets to prevent his escape. The body had then been exhibited before being packed in salt. The superstitious people of the colony arranged for the monstrosity to be burnt, for there was a widespread belief that otherwise it would return to life, and so a huge bonfire was built in a clearing to incinerate the ghastly corpse, but before they could execute their plan, someone approached the men who had killed the three-foot-tall creature, and purchased it for an undisclosed sum. A collector of oddities and curiosities in Liverpool arranged for the Red Gnome's cadaver to be shipped to the home of warehouse keeper, Michael Connolly, at 25 Clarence Street, Everton.

The *Black Hawk* brig carried the curious cargo to Liverpool Docks, and the small cask was delivered – to the wrong Clarence Street ... There were three streets of that name in the city at the time, and instead of going to Everton, it was delivered to the home of Burrows at 25 Clarence Street in the city centre. A servant signed for the cask, and Burrows was horrified when he opened it and was confronted by the grotesque little creature in ragged red clothes, pickled in brine in the barrel. The cask was stored in the cellar, and in the evening when the jeweller went down to show a medical colleague named Ellis the terrifying find – they found the barrel empty and its lid lying on the floor. A trail of pointed footprints led from the puddle of brine up the stairs and out of the cellar.

That evening a fog of unprecedented density descended on the city of Liverpool, and stubbornly refused to lift for over a week. During this time a policeman walked blindly into the Sandon graving dock and drowned, and on the Mersey, ships and steamers collided with one another in the impenetrable murk. While the dense fog prevailed, an irresponsible servant at the jeweller's house, who had overheard the hushed talk of the missing dwarf's corpse, spread the news to her relatives in nearby Pomona Street, and it wasn't long before people in the fogbound neighbourhood were barricading themselves indoors. The resurrected gnome was allegedly spotted in places as far away as Everton and Bootle.

Had someone simply stolen the Red Gnome's corpse from the barrel – or was the real explanation much more sinister?

THE AREA AROUND THE METROPOLITAN CATHEDRAL AND BROWNLOW HILL

Leave Clarence Street on the right side, and then turn right on to Brownlow Hill. Walk up to the Metropolitan Cathedral of Christ the King, and stop when you have crossed Duckinfield Street. On the eastern corner of Duckinfield Street, on the cathedral side, there once stood a house, which in the 1890s, had lain derelict for many years in a dilapidated state ...

THE BROWNLOW HILL VAMPIRE
FROM HAUNTED LIVERPOOL 10

On some nights, the tall, frock-coated silhouette of a nimble male figure was seen to enter and leave the house on the corner of Duckinfield Street, and local legend had it that he was a vampire of incredible age who preyed on people in the nearby Workhouse, which stood on the site now occupied by the great Catholic Cathedral. This vampiric being was suspected by the local populace of living beneath the streets in a vast labyrinth that formed part of the mysterious tunnel network excavated by the Mad Mole of Edge Hill, Joseph Williamson. The vampire went missing for several decades when the house on Duckinfield Street was demolished, but in the 1930s, he apparently returned.

In the 1930s, a family at a house on the corner of Brownlow Hill and Trowbridge Street, were troubled by what they assumed to be rats in their cellar. The Williams family heard a loud scratching sound coming from the cellar on numerous occasions, and so rat catchers were brought in, but caught nothing.

One afternoon, there was a loud crash in the cellar, and when Mr Williams went to investigate, he found a huge gaping hole in the cellar wall, and a pile of crumbled old bricks below it. He summoned his brother, and they both peered into the hole with candles. What they saw amazed them. The hole led to what seemed to be a series of catacombs and tunnels. The Williams brothers knew nothing of the so-called Mole of Edge Hill, and naturally wondered who had constructed the tunnels. They heard the sound of someone breathing heavily nearby, and the faint sounds of footsteps. It sounded like someone large and heavy, and the brothers felt very uneasy, so they fled the tunnel, and bolted back into the cellar. During this time, both men could smell something very similar to altar incense wafting from the tunnels.

The brothers ran upstairs and locked the cellar door, and told a policeman what they had found, and he went to investigate the tunnels later that day with his bull's eye lantern. After a brief exploration of the subterranean passages, the constable returned – white as a sheet. He told Mr Williams that subsidence was to blame, and that the so-called catacombs were nothing more than cellars. He advised him to get the hole bricked up again and left sharpishly. Two of his relatives were bricklayers, so Mr Williams arranged for them to do the job, but halfway through the bricking up, the men heard strange sounds coming from the tunnels. They continued bricking up the hole as quickly as possible, when suddenly, something very powerful punched through the newly set bricks, scattering them everywhere. The bricklayers fled from that cellar as fast as their legs would carry them, and could not be persuaded to go back, even to retrieve their work tools.

Mrs Williams refused to stay in the house alone when her husband went to work, because she thought she had seen a very tall man in black dart across the hall one day towards the cellar. Matters took a sensational turn when an old man in Trowbridge Street claimed that an old vampire was reputed to have his lair beneath Brownlow Hill. The man was much respected in the neighbourhood and was regarded as a very wise old character. He claimed to remember people who had gone missing from the Liverpool Workhouse in the past. A 'thing' was said to appear from under a slab in the bowels of the Workhouse to seize women and children.

Strangely enough, a man who ran Collin's Bookshop on Brownlow Hill confirmed that there had indeed been such a legend. Some said the thing was a ghoul, others claimed it was a vampiric being which lived in a labyrinth of tunnels and chambers under the city. One person in particular was said to know about the strange creature. He was Thomas Whiteside, Catholic Archbishop of Liverpool. He had even sought advice from the Vatican on how to deal with vampires, which are mentioned, or made reference to, in all of the world's cultures. The symbolic eating of bread, representing the body of Christ, and drinking of wine, representing his blood, in the Christian Mass, is thought to echo a much older ritual which had vampiric origins. There were those who said that Archbishop Whiteside had tried and failed to defeat the thing in the tunnels.

Now we go forward to the mid-1960s. The Metropolitan Cathedral was being built on the site of the Workhouse, and the crypt beneath the cathedral was the frequent target of marauding vandals, mostly from Paddington Gardens and the Bullring Tenement. A night watchman named Sugnall was brought in to guard the crypt. In this crypt, which lies deep below the basalt and sandstone of a miniature quarry, there are tombs. There is a vaulted chapel called the Chapel of Relics, and inside there are three large tombs containing the mortal remains of the former Archbishops of Liverpool: Thomas Whiteside, Dr Richard Downey and Dr George Andrew Beck. These tombs are sealed by a gigantic rolling stone, shaped like a disc. It weighs six tons, and requires special machinery to roll it open.

One hot summer evening, the night watchman Sugnall went into the crypt with his Dansette radio and his sandwiches. He sat down in a corner near a small window which had not yet had its glass put in, and he was unwrapping his sandwiches – when he felt the ground shaking beneath his feet. The giant disc-shaped stone was moving, turning slowly anti-clockwise, until a black gaping hole appeared. From this hole walked an abnormally tall figure dressed in black, who slipped into the room where Sugnall was taking his break.

The figure was insubstantial, like a shadow, or a silhouette, and it was heading straight for the night watchman. He couldn't run for the door, because the terrifying figure was blocking the way, so he turned, and in sheer terror and desperation, he tried to scramble through the small hole where the window pane was yet to be fitted. He smashed his head repeatedly against the small opening in his blind panic, and then collapsed from shock and concussion.

When Sugnall came to, the lights were switched off in the crypt, and he had to grope his way to the door. His hand trembled as he fumbled with each of his keys, trying to unlock the door, and as soon as he managed to get it open, he ran for his life. He was later treated for a fractured skull in the Royal Hospital on Pembroke Place. Not surprisingly, Sugnall never returned to his old job, and the authorities blamed vandals for the small amount of damage to the crypt, which was subsequently re-sealed.

Stranger still, that very same week, there was a series of grave robberies in the cemetery of the Anglican Cathedral. All the robberies took place in supposedly impenetrable tombs. Strange men and women in black had been seen in the cathedral cemetery that week, and police even went to the trouble of visiting schools in Edge Hill and Toxteth to advise children to avoid going near the cathedral on their way home. Considering the vast subterranean legacy of the Mole of Edge Hill, and the other uncharted tunnels of Liverpool, could the Brownlow Hill vampire still be at large beneath the city streets?

From the corner of Duckinfield Street, look across the thoroughfare of Brownlow Hill to the street on your left – Great Newton Street.

THE CRYING CHILD

In August 1908, the body of seven-year-old Madge Kirby was dumped in a sack outside 15 Great Newton Street. The child had been abducted in January 1908 by a man who approached her off the Kensington High Street. Over the years since the dreadful murder, a child has been heard crying on Great Newton Street, and some think it is the ghostly sobbing of poor little Madge Kirby's earthbound spirit.

The sad tale of Madge Kirby began in Liverpool at 4.30pm on the wintry afternoon of Monday 6 January 1908. Margaret T Kirby, known affectionately as Madge by her father and friends, was playing near the reservoir in Farnworth Street, Kensington, just around the corner from her home at Number 55 Romily Street. Her father David, thirty-eight, was a plumber, but work had been slow because of his severe depression, caused by the loss of his wife, who had died from a long illness, just a fortnight before.

On that cold afternoon in 1908, as twilight gathered, a man in black clothes approached Madge, who was playing with her best friend Annie McGovern.

"Would you like to come with me for some sweets?" the stranger asked, in a well-spoken voice. He had probably chosen Madge because she was said to have been a child who always stood out amongst her peers because of her exceptional beauty.

Madge nodded innocently, and the sinister man in black took her by the hand and walked away. Madge never returned home for her tea that night, and her father went in search of his daughter without success. He listened with dread when young Annie and her other playmates told him about the man who had accosted Madge with a promise of sweets.

The police lost no time in launching a wide-scale search party for the missing girl. Lakes were dragged, parks scoured, over five thousand empty houses were searched, and there were door-to-door enquiries in Kensington and parts of Edge Hill, but Madge could not be found. Mr Kirby was devastated by the abduction of his daughter, and his sisters and his three-year-old son provided only a modicum of consolation for him. The police asked him to provide a detailed description of his missing daughter so that it could be circulated to police stations throughout Lancashire. Fighting back tears, David told them that Madge had been wearing a black shirt with worn sleeves, a blue pinafore, a black velvet bonnet with black strings, black stockings and laced boots. His beloved daughter had brown hair, sky-blue eyes and a very fair and fresh-faced complexion.

In St Michael's School, which Madge Kirby had attended, the teachers and children said prayers each day for the missing girl's safe return. The months wore on, but still no trace of Madge could be found – until eight months later, on the morning of Tuesday, 21 August, when a man going to work came upon a sack on Great Newton Street, off London Road. That sack contained the remains of a scantily clad girl. The body of Madge Kirby had been found at last. Now the hunt was on for her killer.

Madge's body was found in a dry onion sack on the rainy pavement outside a condemned house at Number 15 Great Newton Street, near London Road. A subsequent investigation determined that the sack had been kept in the cellar of the derelict house. The police lost no time in launching a murder hunt, but their investigations were largely obstructed by the public. Crowds of people congregated like ghouls outside Prescot Street Police Station, eager to hear of the latest developments in the shocking murder case.

On the night after the body was found, two policemen rushed out of the police station with a bloodhound leading the way. The dog led the officers in a western direction, and the great mob followed – six people raced after the police on bicycles, two elderly men were pushed along in their wheelchairs, and several women even pushed prams as they joined in the hunt. Over two thousand people poured down Prescot Street, many of them carrying refreshments, towards the city centre, but little did they know that the bloodhound they were following was but a decoy.

Shortly after midnight, one of the most astounding bloodhounds ever to be deployed by the Lancashire Constabulary emerged from the police station and immediately took up the scent he'd taken from the clothes of the murdered child. His name was Czar, a very sensitive dog who had been loaned from a Mr Pakenham. Czar took the police on a curious trail that wound through the Botanic Gardens, then on to a strip of secluded wasteground on the eastern extremities of Edge Lane. From there, Czar led the constables to Tunnel Road, and on to Edge Hill Railway Station. Czar dragged the policeman to the city centre-bound platform and stood stock still, gazing at the tunnel. He convulsed, and sniffed the air. That tunnel led directly to Lime Street. Czar was bundled into a horse-drawn cab, and the cab-driver was instructed to go to Lime Street Railway Station, where the bloodhound bolted straight for Platform One. Czar barked and howled at the tunnel, and the dog's owner said that he believed this meant that Madge Kirby's killer had left Liverpool for the Midlands, as trains from that platform were bound for Birmingham.

There, the tantalising trail went cold. Weird gloating letters bearing a London postmark, from 'The King of Darkness' were sent to the Liverpool detective assigned to the child murder case. The author of the letters was evidently a malevolent and deranged individual, but the letters provided no clue to the identity of the murderer, or of any possible motive.

On Great Newton Street, witnesses talked of a foreign-looking man in black who had been seen loitering near the house where Madge's body was later found. Other people in the area claimed this man had visited the yard of that house dressed in women's clothes. Unfortunately, the case still remains unsolved.

Walk up Brownlow Hill, and climb the steps to the great square of the Metropolitan Cathedral. This square is said to be haunted by the ghost of a ragged-clothed man, and around 1971, a suicidal man had a chilling encounter with the spectre.

BERNIE WITH THE BROKEN NECK
FROM HAUNTED LIVERPOOL 1

This incident allegedly took place shortly before Christmas, one snowy night in the 1970s. It was one o'clock in the morning and Brownlow Hill was deserted. A light dusting of snow was falling and settling on the ground, but one person who was out at that hour seemed unaffected by the chilly weather. Mr Smith, a young Liverpool businessman, walked up the flights of steps in Brownlow Hill that lead to the Metropolitan Cathedral's main square. As he reached the top of the icy steps, his footsteps echoed in the silence.

The businessman stopped in his tracks and took out his keys. He lovingly clutched the keyring given to him by his wife just three short years ago. Mr Smith had stopped at the very place where he and Melanie had walked on the night of their first date. He had met her at the Augustus John pub when they had both been students at Liverpool University. He had always been sceptical about true love until he met Melanie. She had moved into his flat and they married less than a year later. Tragedy closely followed, when Melanie died from a brain tumour and it hurt Mr Smith to think of his wife's terrible suffering in the weeks before her death. Still unable to come to terms with the loss of Melanie, he found himself on this freezing December morning at the very spot where he had once been so happy.

With leaden legs, Mr Smith climbed on to the snow-covered wall that bordered the square and prepared himself to jump down into the crypt, some fifty feet below. Life was unbearable without Melanie, and he could not face spending another Christmas without her. He closed his eyes and was about to jump when someone shouted out behind him. He looked around in surprise, having thought he was completely alone.

"Don't!" shouted a scruffy-looking man standing in the square behind him and he held out his arms to the would-be suicide.

"Shut up! Beat it!" Mr Smith warned him and started to cry.

The tramp stood his ground.

"No, I won't. It isn't right. Just because your little world is falling apart. That's the coward's way out!"

Mr Smith shouted a string of four-letter words and ended, "I don't want to live, so just leave me alone."

"Okay, friend, but have you ever wondered what will become of you if you do decide to jump?"

"Yes," said Mr Smith, "I'll be dead, that's what'll become of me."

"A child knows that," persisted the tramp, "but what if that isn't the end?"

"You're drunk, just leave me alone," snapped Smith and he turned back to look at the glistening ground below.

"You mightn't even die if you fall down there," the tramp persisted.

"Just go, will you?"

The tramp stayed put and rambled on, "You could smash your head in and end up like a cabbage. You'll have to be spoon-fed."

Mr Smith took a deep breath and started to sway back and forth slightly.

"Even if you smash your brains in and your organs fly everywhere, you might still take a few minutes to die," added the tramp, "and you know when you're lying there after the fall and you're barely alive, all your organs are ruptured and your blood is spreading into a great big puddle, you taste your own salty blood in your mouth and you are seized by this terrible panic and you change your mind and suddenly want to live. You hope and wish that it's all just a bad dream – but it isn't. You realise with horror that you're going to die."

"And how do you know all this?" Mr Smith asked the tramp, suddenly diverted from his own misery.

"I'll give you a clue," grinned the tramp and tilted his head until his ear touched his shoulder.

Mr Smith shuddered when he saw the tramp's contortion act. Surely he was just double-jointed. The tramp then flipped his head right back in one swift, unnatural movement, so that the back of his head actually touched his shoulder blades. With a sense of mounting horror, Mr Smith realised that no one – not even someone who was double-jointed – could flip his head back like that. The tramp turned around on the spot and his dangling head swung about as if his neck was broken.

With his face upside down, he smiled, "I jumped. Look what happened."

Mr Smith got down off the wall, trembling, and ran across the square in a state of fear and confusion. He turned back once and saw that the tramp had vanished. The businessman then hesitated and looked down at the snow. He could clearly see his own trail of footprints but could see no trace of footprints leading to the spot where the vagrant had appeared. Mr Smith hurried down the steps two at a time and raced up Brownlow Hill. It had stopped snowing and a full moon had emerged from a break in the clouds. He glanced backwards once again towards the Cathedral and saw a solitary, shadowy figure coming down the steps in the moonlight. He could not be sure, but the figure looked like the tramp with the broken neck. Horrified, he realised that it was heading his way. He was relieved to find a black hackney cab which took him safely back to his home in Old Swan.

The chilling experience left Mr Smith with no further desires to end his life and he gradually pulled himself out of his depression.

In the February of the following year, he read an interesting article in the *Liverpool Echo* that stated that a group of tourists visiting the Metropolitan Cathedral had encountered the ghost of a shabby-looking man in the Cathedral's main square. After smiling at the Americans, the man vanished before their startled eyes. A ghosthunter looked into the case and found that many other people had seen the same solid-looking phantom of a bedraggled figure. A medium who was brought in to make contact with the ghost, claimed that the apparition was Bernie Brown, who had died in the Liverpool Workhouse in the nineteenth century after breaking his neck jumping from a window. This seemed to fit, because the Cathedral was built on the site of the old Liverpool Workhouse. So take a good look around you and watch out for Bernie with the broken neck!

Staying on the same side of Brownlow Hill as the cathedral, walk up to the corner, where Mount Pleasant joins the road, opposite the redbrick and terracotta University Clock Tower. Three supernatural incidents have allegedly taken place here.

THE HEADLESS PRIEST

In 2004, a headless priest was seen by many witnesses, walking up Mount Pleasant, opposite Mountford Hall, towards Brownlow Hill. At the time of these terrifying sightings, the old Diocesan Council Office was being demolished, and so it is possible that the headless ghost was that of a former Catholic priest.

Now walk back down Brownlow Hill for just a few yards. The building now standing to your left was erected on the site of the Diocesan Council Office.

PRIESTS IN LIMBO

In December 1986, two Catholic priests, Father Howard and Father Andrew, came out of the Diocesan Council Office at about five minutes to five in the afternoon. Father Howard was the older priest, and Father Andrews was twenty-five. As the priests walked up the street on their way to a bookshop called Parry's Books, they suddenly noticed that things had become unusually quiet. Not a single person passed them, and there were no cars on the road, even though it was rush hour. The priests walked into the bookshop and found the place deserted. The cash registers were operational and the place was lit up, yet there was no one about. Not a single member of staff, or any customers. This obviously made the priests uneasy. They waited and waited, but no one came into the place, and there was no one outside to be seen either. Father Andrews nervously joked, "Perhaps there's a bomb scare on and everyone's been evacuated."

The time seemed to drag by, and when Father Howard glanced out of the bookshop window at the university clocktower, he was amazed to see that the time was still five minutes to five. It was almost as if the clock had stopped. Father Andrew tapped on the door of the staffroom in the bookshop, but there was no answer. When he looked inside, he saw handbags and coats and other items belonging to the staff, but no sign of any assistants. It was a scene more reminiscent of the *Mary Celeste* than of a city centre bookshop.

According to Father Andrews, the baffled priests then went next door to a pub called the Augustus John, and to their horror, found the premises there deserted as well. The one-armed bandits were illuminated and the bar and lounge were lit up, yet no one was about.

Feeling very unsettled and perplexed, the two priests decided to hurry back to the Diocesan Council building on Brownlow Hill. Halfway through their journey, Father Andrews said, "I don't like this one bit."

"I think it's the other fella up to his tricks," joked the elder priest, referring to the Devil, suddenly adding, "Jesus, please get us out of this situation."

At that precise moment, a vagrant who was well known in the area came around the corner from the direction of the Students Union building. Then the two priests heard the screeching sound of a bus's pneumatic brakes. When they turned round there was traffic on Brownlow Hill again and then they heard the clocktower striking five o'clock.

The priest who told me about this strange incident showed me his old diary for December 1986, and there was a full account written down, exactly as he had told me. The other priest who now lives down south, also confirmed the weird story.

"It was as if we had strolled into Limbo that day," Father Howard reflected with a shudder.

Walk across Brownlow Hill to the Victoria Building, with the university clock overhead. Since the 1970s, a very strange apparition – that of a black Rolls Royce with a devilish passenger – has been seen to appear at the traffic lights here, apparently out of nowhere.

THE BLACK ROLLS ROYCE

This part of the city is a notorious red-light district, and over the years, many ladies of the night, as well as innocent women returning from city centre clubs, have told again and again of seeing the black Rolls Royce appear out of nowhere, and how its door would open to reveal a Mephistophelian figure sitting in the rear of the vehicle. The sinister man with the Van Dyke beard and gleaming red eyes, invites the women into the luxurious car, and if they refuse he curses them and the Rolls either vanishes immediately, or fades away as it cruises up towards Paddington.

One young prostitute recalled how she unwisely accepted a ride in the Rolls Royce. As she was climbing into the vehicle she realised that she was taking a stupid risk, but she was beguiled by the plush leather seats and the gleaming metalwork. She became convinced that the strange, well-dressed passenger was the Devil himself, for he seemed to know all her innermost secrets and every incident of her life. She ended up scrambling out of the vehicle in abject terror to the laughter of the demonic passenger and his shadowy chauffeur.

Now walk down Brownlow Hill, towards the town centre, until you come to the Adelphi Hotel on your left. Two ghosts are said to haunt this once magnificent hotel.

HAUNTINGS AT THE ADELPHI

One of these ghosts is a young, almost transparent lady who, for some peculiar reason, rifles through the jackets of hotel guests in the dead of night.

When Winston Churchill stayed at the hotel in the 1930s, he was said to have been awakened in the wee small hours by this female ghost, who was muttering something unintelligible as she searched through his belongings. The ghost melted into the night as soon as Churchill spoke to it.

The other ghost is that of a man who committed suicide at the hotel in the 1930s. He haunts the upper floors and has been described as a tall, dark man dressed in a tuxedo, with a pencil moustache and slicked back hair. He has been sighted on numerous occasions, gazing out of the hotel windows on to Brownlow Hill, and even shouting to passers by.

LEWIS'S CORNER

Cross Mount Pleasant and walk towards Renshaw Street. Cross Renshaw Street, then turn right and walk until you come to Lewis's Corner, on Ranelagh Place. Above you stands the statue entitled Liverpool Resurgent, also known locally as 'Dickie Lewis'.

STOOD UP

This corner has always been a favourite rendezvous for blind dates and a meeting place for lovers. In the late 1950s, a woman waited in vain here for a date who never arrived. Most people would have been hurt by being stood up, but she was already deeply depressed and it proved to be the final straw. Feeling utterly worthless and dejected, she went home, poured herself a bath and slit her wrists.

Her ghost, dressed in black and wearing a pillbox hat, was often seen standing under the statue with a pale morose face in the 1960s.

CENTRAL STATION

Turn into Ranelagh Street, back towards Central Station, where we began the Ghost Walk, but before you enter the station, look right, across the road towards the Midland Hotel pub, a Grade II listed building which dates back to 1875.

THE UMBRELLA MAN

One rainy afternoon in the late summer of 1900, a handful of drinkers in the Midland Hotel on Ranelagh Street were being entertained by an outlandishly dressed black banjo player known as the Ethiopian Minstrel. With his stars and stripes top hat, yellow frock coat, embroidered waistcoat and gold lamé trousers, the Minstrel was a sight to behold. He had the voice of an opera singer, with an incredible range and distinctive timbre.

The Ethiopian finished his songs, went round collecting with his hat and then prepared to leave the public house. A flash of lightning lit up Ranelagh Street, followed by a heavy roll of thunder and a vicious downpour. Moments later, the door of the saloon swung open and in came Mr Antonio, the local 'ice-cream johnnie' whose gaily decorated barrow was parked outside on Cases Street. He handed the minstrel a cone of Neapolitan ice-cream and ordered a gin for himself. The ice cream vendor complained about the dreadful weather which was ruining his business.

Seconds after Mr Antonio had arrived, a tall stranger, dressed in black, also came into the pub, clutching half a dozen umbrellas. He asked if anybody wanted one of the brollies, and most of the drinkers shook their heads – that is until the man said that he wanted nothing for them.

When the minstrel set eyes upon this stranger, his eyes widened, and he backed away, then hurried out of the pub. People noticed his behaviour and obviously thought it was strange. When the man had given out all the umbrellas, several drinkers asked him why the street musician had scarpered. The man just smiled and said nothing in reply. He too silently left the pub and disappeared into the sheets of rain.

The umbrellas which the odd man had given away were all black, and their handles were adorned with a very unusual feature – a small human skull fashioned out of metal. Antonio, who was very superstitious, was convinced that there was something evil about the umbrellas, but a railway guard named Williams laughed at the idea and argued that the man in black had just been some eccentric – the city was full of them he said.

However, Mr Antonio's instinct proved to be correct. The railway guard suffered horrific nightmares each night from that day on, and a month later, he hanged himself after apparently suffering from a nervous breakdown.

The five other people who had taken one of the umbrellas all started suffering from vivid, heart-stopping nightmares, and one by one, over the space of six months, each of them met their death. One boarded a ship called the *Primrose Hill* and drowned after it was wrecked on rocks at Holyhead, another died of influenza, and a woman who owned one of the umbrellas passed away as she gave birth to her child. The remaining person was a Londoner, and he died in a fire in the East End.

When the Ethiopian Minstrel returned to the Midland pub a year later, he was not surprised by the news of the deaths, as he had come across the man who gave the cursed umbrellas away many times before in other pubs, and believed him to be the Devil himself.

"Did none of you notice his small feet?" the Minstrel asked, "They were cloven feet. The Devil comes in many ingenious disguises, but he always betrays some imperfection."

The Minstrel seemed to be talking with authority and a chill ran up everyone's spine when they heard this pronouncement.